HEAL YOUR SH!T FIND YOUR HAPPY

HEAL YOUR SH!T FIND YOUR HAPPY

Get Into Your Body
Break the Cycle
of Generational Trauma

CHRISTINE VARNAVAS

ISBN: 978-1-958150-16-0
Heal Your Sh!t Find Your Happy
Get Into Your Body Break the Cycle of Generational Trauma

Paperpack
May 2023

Subjects:
FAMILY & RELATIONSHIPS / Abuse / Child Abuse
SELF-HELP / Post-Traumatic Stress Disorder (PTSD)
SELF-HELP / Personal Growth / Happiness

Published by Inner Peace Press
Eau Claire, Wisconsin, USA
www.innerpeacepress.com

To my family, friends, and teachers.
Past, present, and future.
You know who you are. I love you.

Table of Contents

Foreword

According to the National Council on Behavioral Health, 70% of adults in the United States have experienced trauma at least once in their lifetime that is 223.4 million people. *Heal Your Sh!t Find Your Happy: Get Into Your Body Break the Cycle of Generational Trauma* is a must read book based on Christine's own lived experiences of trauma, unrealized generational trauma, and epigenetic and scientific research.

As someone who had a front-row seat to much of Christine's story, I found myself transfixed to the pages. Christine's story is one that not only informs the mind but also the heart. It is an amazing book to keep close to you, to return to repeatedly, whether you are healing or, like I am, in the profession of helping others to heal, this book is for you.

Dr. Amy Schlieve
SCHLIEVE CONSULTING

Introduction

L et me start by saying... thank you! First to my mom and my two amazing daughters who have taught me so much. I love you.

Secondly, to all the amazing beings who have been with me on this wicked wonderful journey of self-discovery, healing, moving, laughing, face-planting, getting back up again, learning how things work and more. You've been with me through re-inventing myself (many times), two marriages, two divorces, two child births, two miscarriages, a car accident, knee surgeries, my first attempt at college, college and graduate school, many fitness and yoga certifications, hangovers, countless beautiful vacations to Greece, and much, much more. You've been there all along and I'm so grateful. I love you all!

I'm writing this to offer hope, healing, and as a call to action for women to heal your shit now so you can stop the chain of pain for future generations.

This is dedicated to all adult women who are sexual assault survivors. For those of you out there who keep going and pushing through your stress mess even when you feel like you can't breathe. For those who got up on days when you didn't think you could, had children when you didn't think you could or should, were brave enough to face accusers head on, regardless of the outcome. For those who have lived through childhood trauma, who constantly second guess themselves, who belong to the "What's Wrong With Me? Club", who've yelled at people they love or over reacted so hard it caused them to wonder if they were losing their mind, and simultaneously didn't understand why they acted that way.

And for those of us who are part of the Shame Club... because of what we did, said, or othered to those we love and then felt like shit for days, months, or years about it.

Healing is the missing key to helping you feel better and to stop the cycle of madness.

If we heal our shit in this lifetime, it minimizes the impact of shit we pass on to the next generation whether it's your children or grandchildren or great great great... you get the picture... We do the work now to help future generations suffer less.

Sounds a little like playing God? Maybe, but if you do the work in this body, in this life, on this planet, at this time, it will have a positive impact on the future and help ease suffering for generations to come.

It doesn't get any bigger than that.

Also, to all the moms or other adult figures who love someone who's been hurt as a child, a few key things: the assault never goes away, it's woven into our being, stored in our bodies and our minds forever, especially if we don't process it out. When the amazing being you love, who has been hurt, reacts out of proportion to the situation, yells, is overwhelmed easily, is depressed or anxious, or on and on and on... PLEASE take a moment to understand what childhood trauma can do to some of us. I say some, because not all of us are affected the same way. In my case, my childhood trauma hijacked my nervous system (my internal processing center... thoughts, feelings, emotions, etc.), which made me think, act, and feel a certain way. I didn't understand it and I'm pretty certain those around me didn't either.

Just please know that understanding how stress and trauma work from a neurophysiological (brain/body) standpoint is an explanation, not an excuse. Explanations are those golden nuggets that can soften gnarly situations. We didn't ask for what happened to us, BUT it is our responsibility to navigate how we show up in this life despite the situation.

I ask that you amplify your curiosity. That will go a long way and be appreciated.

Most of us, unless we are medically trained or have professional training and/or work in the mental health field, are not aware of how trauma works. The word trauma is becoming more mainstream and I believe we (as a country in the U.S.) are beginning to understand that trauma is not isolated to the battlefield. It is an equal opportunity experience that can and does affect everyone.

The impact that the assault had on me was that it hijacked and preconditioned my **autonomic nervous system** (built-in safety system – fight or flight, rest and digest, freeze and fawn) to be on high alert all the time and default to the fight or flight (protect) response and freeze and fawn. Not the rest and digest response (connect).

The assault was the catalyst to my system, defaulting to a fear-based mode (protect) when life happened as it does. It was the precursor to how I (my nervous system) would react to (manage) stressful situations in the future.

Lastly, be gentle with those you love. They are not trying to be an asshole. No one, at least no one I know, wakes up one morning and says, "I think I'll be an asshole today," or "I feel bad, so I'll make the people around me feel bad too." Chances are they are overwhelmed and it's their *trauma drama* that is showing up.

Trauma drama is a phrase I made up when I was trying to explain to my clients how their unresolved childhood trauma can show up in their adult lives. Unprocessed trauma can cause relentless drama for the person who's carrying it to themselves and those around them.

Healing is work. It doesn't necessarily always have to be hard and painful. But it does require having the right support, the right tools, and a plan to act.

I created a mantra years ago once I started on the healing path. "Do my work. Do good work. Do no harm." It has helped.

The stories I share in this book are not meant to foster a sense of victimhood. They are simply meant to show you a path I chose when at other times choice was not an option.

This is written to offer hope. To show that healing can and does happen. It does not happen overnight. It also does not have to suck all the time. You will cry. You will laugh. You may even have fun.

So let's create an actionable plan for how to live and co-create the world we want to live in. Who's with me?

> "Women are emotionally and physically stressed.
> Look at this culture between the two major genders.
> Which is the one that's programmed by this particular
> culture to take care of others emotionally while ignoring
> their own needs… told to identify with their duties
> rather than the needs of the self… taught not to be
> angry, they must repress their anger… made to feel
> responsible for how other people feel. There's more
> autoimmune disease among women. The more stress
> and the more social oppression people experience the
> greater the risk for these conditions."
> - Gabor Maté, Physician, Addiction Expert, Author

How The Story Came Out
&
Why Women Don't Tell

the repercussions
and the reality
of telling

Allow me to recall how the story of my sexual assault came out.

From what I remember… I was 16 and a junior in high school. It would have been 1981… maybe. I graduated in 1983 so… The current boy I was in deep lust with was home on leave from the Marines. He was part of a group of boys from "the other high school" I had met with a friend. I don't remember how we met them, but there were three of them. We ended up spending a lot of time together. We drank a lot. It's Wisconsin. We had fun. We hung out at each other's houses… well their houses. Not mine.

I ended up having a "short thing" with one of them, but that ended when I walked in and caught him and my friend going at it on her living room floor. Oh hormones…

One of the others was "the Marine." He was for all purposes the leader of the pack and I really liked him. I was attracted to his confidence. He drove a cool car, he was fairly good looking, and his family was amazing.

I don't remember how or why I started spending time with his family but his mother and I clicked right away. I started spending a lot of time with her. She once told me I was the daughter she never had. Well, let's boost my teen ego a bit. Yes, please, more of this.

His family liked me. They wanted me around. This feeling was so new to me that I felt like I'd won the lottery. His mom, his dad, and his brother all liked me. It was a whole family unit. They wanted me around. It was like a drug. It felt so good.

It felt good to be wanted. Not just by the guys you just sleep with and really secretly like a lot more than they like you because you feel worthless all the time and if they pay attention to you, you might not be the worthless piece of shit you really feel like you are. Yup, that's a thing!

Translation? They liked me, so I must NOT be a worthless piece of shit. They wanted me around. They invited me to do "family things."

We spent hours at their house hanging out at the kitchen table playing cards and ultimately they invited me to go "camping" with them. I'd never done that before. I'd never had a family who sat at the kitchen table and who ate a meal together and played cards or who "went camping."

Our family meals in my house were eating and watching TV or my brother Kevin and I eating a TV dinner together on the floor of the family room and watching TV. There was a lot of TV in my life. I was a kid of the 80s.

Camping for this family was not what I knew as camping. There was no tent. My experience with camping was as a girl scout at Girl Scout camp at camp Adahi in the Tennessee Mountains. We slept in tents on cots. We cooked our food over a fire. We hiked. We rode horses. We did crafts.

Camping to them was driving an hour or so to their "camper," setting up the camper from the last time it was used, emptying the truck with all the stuff that was needed to camp, and then the fun started. Eating, drinking beer, playing cards, and going to the bar to drink more.

I ended up going camping many, many times with this family. I loved it. The mom and dad and I bonded in a way that was probably not very healthy at times looking back. But I loved every minute of it... well almost every minute.

The mom was lovely. She loved me and made a point of telling me all the time. The dad was tall and what I imagined my dad looked like (I met my dad later in life) and I loved him dearly. He'd call me "The Greek" or "kid" or other names that made me feel special, wanted, and cared about.

They both wanted their oldest son and I to be a couple. His mom talked about it a lot in my presence.

I'm pretty sure he, the son, had no idea how deep the relationship between his family and I had gotten. His brother and I were friends. We were closer in age. Both boys were adopted and this family was a very tight unit.

It felt like I was part of something for the first time since I left Tennessee. Part of a family that wanted me around and they had fun. I had fun with them. Keep in mind here that this is not me saying my family did not want me around. That was never part of the equation, it just felt so good to be actively wanted. Notice I've said the word fun here a few times.

When we were camping, we ate together, we sat at the fire at night listening to music, drinking a lot of beer, listening to country music, laughing, and talking about their son, the Marine, who was away.

When I wasn't camping with them, I often spent time at their house, sitting in the kitchen, eating, talking, and sharing news from letters from their son who was far far away in California. The world seemed like a much bigger place back then.

I laugh now, at "far far away" because this was a pre-internet world; a pre-e-mail world. We were still writing letters. It feels like forever ago.

So that's who he was and why the "how I told my mom" story is such a big deal. Their son was home on leave when the story officially came out. His being home on leave was a huge deal because his family and I had talked about it forever. It was like it was a national holiday and to his parents it was. Plus he and I had been writing to each other and he wanted to see me when he got back. It was a huge deal. My need to be wanted was also a huge deal.

How my story came out... or how I told my mother... was the beginning of years of trauma drama and stress and was short of a landslide. Actually, it was more like a volcano erupting.

So, "the Marine" was home. I don't remember how involved we were the last time he was home. I'm pretty sure that our entire relationship evolved around the letter writing and his mom cheering us on to be a couple.

Anyway, he was home on leave and it was a BIG DEAL. I was still in high school. I was a junior and had a strict curfew.

I really don't remember what happened that evening other than he and I ended up spending a lot of time together and I didn't care what time it was. He was paying attention to me.

Eventually he drove me home in his infamous shiny bright blue 19-something-or-other Chevy Malibu that was his version of a child. He loved that car and talked about it as if it was a living being. Cars were not a big deal in my family so this was very odd to me, but I didn't care, because it was him and he was amazing to me.

We sat in front of my house in this car and made out. I felt like I'd died and gone to heaven. I can't remember if he was a good kisser or not. Which may say something. Ha! But I'm pretty sure I didn't care then. He was home. His family who loved me were ecstatic at his being home and he was kissing me. Life was perfect.

Well, until it wasn't and my mom came outside... I got out of the car and she slapped me on the face. She'd only done that one time before when I was younger, at which time I promptly responded by slamming a swinging door so hard that it came off the hinges.

This time I'd stayed out way past my curfew. I'd just gotten home from staying out all night. I mean all night. I'd never done that. I have no idea what happened immediately following that; however the slap and the emotion it triggered was the precursor to the major volcanic eruption of the story coming out.

I was grounded! That was a given.

It was a Saturday or Sunday morning (funny how some things are set in stone and others are fluzzy – as my girls used to say when they were younger). I was sitting outside on our front steps. Probably smoking since I wasn't allowed to smoke in the house – smart mom. Mom was inside vacuuming the living room. I was livid that she grounded me while he was home on leave. I stomped in the house and began yelling, or screaming, which is probably more accurate.

I can still feel the impact of these words coming out of my mouth. I very eloquently and violently screamed...

almost as if it'd been scripted, "I'd rather live with Rick and put up with his sexual abuse than live here with you, knowing (insert name here) is home on leave and I can't see him!"

Holy shit! Imagine your daughter coming in and yelling this at you.

She froze.

The surreal part of this is that I was raging clearly, but I had no idea that this was going to come out of my mouth. I was just raging or spewing or going postal or whatever you want to call it.

It felt like a volcano erupted inside of me and then it spewed all over my mom and our living room and the vacuum and any other objects in its way. Anything in the foreseeable area was the recipient of the lava and its orange glowing thick liquid lethal mess.

As I said, she froze. I don't remember the look on her face, but I have a vague memory (more like a sense) of her appearing shocked, stunned, and being in disbelief. Not disbelief of what I'd just said, but disbelief that I was yelling this at her as if it were her fault. Which it clearly was not.

I was furious with her for grounding me and I wanted her to know it and in my stressed out, fight or flight, hormone filled, teen brain, I needed her to know just how mad I was at her. Keep in mind, the feeling of being furious with her and the volcanic eruption happened simultaneously. They were both visceral, related but not connected... or so I thought.

I don't have a memory of thinking "does she believe me or not?" She immediately believed me.

She asked me if I'd "ever told" her this before. I said no. She'd recently taken a class on child abuse and had learned the "why some children don't report – they are not believed."

Rick, my adopted father, had a history of "messing around with his female college students." So I'm fairly certain this wasn't a stretch for her to believe what I shared.

SIDE NOTE:

THIS IS VERY IMPORTANT! When I say "she immediately believed me" is a golden nugget here because had she not, my life would have been dangerously different. She always believed me. I am very grateful for that.

WHY IS THIS IMPORTANT? Because over the years, as I shared my story with other women, I learned that I was not the norm. I've had many women trust me with their stories and I learned that most of them WERE NOT BELIEVED. Or they never told anyone up until recently, are suffering in life and are questioned by others as to WHY they are just now telling what happened to them.

Most of the women who were brave enough to tell their moms or other adult female caregivers were told that "it never happened." Most of these brave women have had their stories turned back on them (BLAME THE VICTIM) or denied that it ever happened... Insert eye roll and shaking head here.

This is the denial or the blame and shame the victim shit that has been going on for centuries. And it's bullshit. Let's just call it what it is. It's bullshit. We all know these stories happen behind closed doors all the time.

And my heart goes out to those who have shared their stories in confidence or with the hope that the person they are telling will and or can do something about it... I'm speaking in reference to children who tell.

As a child, to be so brave to share a gross and ugly story, without maybe even having the words to describe what happened to them, give details of an event they don't even understand, and then to have the adult listening to flip or deny the story just adds salt to the wound and can re-traumatize the child, who tired to self-advocate.

Back to what happened next... Mom asked me to repeat it. I did. I felt numb. I felt rage. I felt betrayed. I felt disbelief. I was having *all* the feelings. But, at the same time, I was completely present and aware of what was happening. I was there witnessing all of this coming out of my mouth and a little shocked that it was happening at the same time. Almost as if it was happening to someone else and I was just part of the scene.

There is a short period of time that I don't remember immediately following my explosion. I'm pretty certain she asked me questions and I answered as best as I could in a semi calmed down rage state.

What I do remember is us leaving the living room and going into my bedroom and sitting on the floor and her calling him on the phone.

He answered. She told him what I'd said.

Wait for it…

Wait for it…

Wait for it…

He said, and I quote (because I'll NEVER forget this), "Carolyn, I'm going out of town and I'll call you when I get back."

"WHAT… are you f—-g kidding me?" or something similar is what I was thinking at the time.

Yup! That's what he said. My mom was still in shock. I could tell by the blank look and profound confusion on her face as she repeated it to me, as if to say, "That's what he said, he didn't deny it, he just calmly said…" and then she repeated again what he said.

I'm pretty sure what I saw happen next was my mom going into problem solving mode. Her problem solving skills are exceptional. The next person she called was her attorney in Tennessee.

That began a lawsuit she filed on my behalf as I was a minor.

From that point on the trauma drama began. The lawsuit, the bullshit, the denials, the family drama, and anger from his mother towards me, his brother disowning me (someone I'd worshiped as an uncle and loved dearly), and more began to take shape and be an underlying current in our lives for what felt like forever.

It went on for roughly three years.

It was a nightmare at times… meaning, he denied it. Of course he did. What else was he going to do? He retained an attorney. He had a public image to uphold as Dr. Wilson, the longtime Political Science Professor at the University of Tennessee at Chattanooga. He was a Fulbright Professor who often taught in China, a local Politician, and an author. He was probably scared shitless about his secret getting out. Or in denial.

There are a few things that stand out that I do remember very clearly from the fall out of the "it getting out" story.

First, it went to court in Chattanooga, where he lived. He was friends with the judge (of course he was). I was told that the judge looked at the case (or file) and immediately dismissed it because then (I'm not sure if it's changed now), in 1980-something, a minor COULD NOT SUE a parent in the state of Tennessee.

The judge literally threw the case out.

I've watched enough legal TV shows in my 50 some years that I have this visual of a white male judge in robes, sitting on his bench, which is, of course, elevated from the floor, looking through a pile of files, mine's on the top of the pile. He grabs it. Sees that the case title is Wilson (I was a Wilson then because he adopted me) versus Wilson. He opens it and reads further and sees on the front page that it's a "minor suing a parent," and it stops there… he goes no further to see what the case REALLY is about and thinks "Nope, not allowed." He then puts it in the "Nope" file pile and goes on with the rest of the stack.

That's the visual I get and have seen played out over and over and over in my head for decades, just like a TV show, but it wasn't a TV show. It was my life happening and it was unfair. Believe me, little me, teenage me, and all the other versions of me, have had a "it's not fair" mantra etched in my bones since this injustice took place.

The reality is I really have no idea how that all played out. I just know that the judge threw it out.

However, what happened next is pretty big. The attorney on the case appealed the ruling. It then went to the 6th Circuit Court of Appeals in 1984… and I won! I made legal history.* Well the case won. We (Mom and I) were nowhere near close to getting resolution, amends, or closure.

The reach and the tendrils that this story has had and continues to have, including the numbers of people it affected then and now (almost 50 years later), and how it

* https://law.justia.com/cases/federal/appellate-courts/F2/742/1004/213045/

continues to play out in my life, in my daughters' lives, and in my brother's children's lives is ridiculous at best.

It affected everyone in Rick's immediate family. It affected my family. And it's affected my daughters who weren't even born until 30 years later. This is mind boggling. Let's start with the lawsuit itself and what I remember before jumping into how it affects my family today.

The lawsuit, once his family was made aware of it, caused a ripple effect that I, at the brilliant age of 16, could never have foreseen.

Two things as I said earlier stand out to me the most. The winter after the lawsuit was filed, we (Mom, Kevin, and I) were in southern Minnesota staying with my grandparents (Mom's parents). Both sets of grandparents lived in the same town, and, how convenient, that in a town of only 10,000 people, they lived across the street from each other!

As was customary when we arrived in town, Kevin and I would go to both houses, say hi, and love on the grandparents. Mom and Rick were married when I was three-years-old. So I don't really remember a time when his parents weren't my grandparents.

First, as per my usual, I ran into the house and hugged my grandma and grandpa, and then I went across the street to Rick's parents house to say hi.

As I walked in the side door of his parents' house attached to the driveway, as I'd done dozens of times over the years, his mom met me at the top of the steps that went to her kitchen. She was a tall woman and was towering over me, standing on the inside steps. She was blocking me from entering the house any further and began yelling at me. Her words are still burned in my brain all these years later. "All you do is take, take, take. How could you do this? How could you hurt me like this? I'll never forgive you!"

I immediately felt like I was two feet tall and five years old as opposed to 16 years old and five feet and eight inches. I froze (seems to be a pattern here). I was in shock and couldn't believe she was saying this to me. I had no skills or experience with anything like this so I had no place to hang it mentally. I'd never been spoken to like this by an adult.

Clearly I had hurt her, but at that time (in my 16 year old brain) I couldn't comprehend the magnitude of this. She was an adult, and my grandma. Why would she not believe me?

I was shocked. I was hurt. I was confused. I was later angry. I ended up telling my friends who lived there. They were shocked, too, because they'd heard the story (sort of) and knew her well. These two best childhood friends (from that same town) and I had gone to his parents' cabin in the summers and had amazing fun for many years.

I can't imagine what was going on in her head at the time. I had "outed" and accused her son publicly of being a child molester. She obviously took it as a personal attack and lashed out at me. Looking back now, over the years I recognize that as she was living in a small town, working in a school, she would be afraid of what would happen once the news made it around town. Her husband was also a local business owner so they were fairly well known.

My response to her verbal attack was to tell my friends and then promptly go write the word BITCH in big letters in the snow in her yard. It felt good, but I also knew in that moment that it would come back to haunt me. It did.

The other thing that happened on his family's side is that it ended, for many years, my relationship with his brother. He and I were never in the same space for too long, but, when we were, we connected, we played, and I loved him like he was the big brother I never had. I loved him. I trusted him. I felt safe with him.

That ended when the story came out. He stopped talking to me and my mom. We didn't see him for years. The teenage me desperately wanted him to believe me and just hear my side of the story. I tried once to talk to him on the phone to tell him I was sorry for what this had done to the family, and that I needed him to believe me. Why would I make this up?

I also knew how hard it must have been for him to hear those things.

But he wouldn't or couldn't… I don't know. I remember feeling like that hurt more than what his brother did to me. It still sometimes makes me cry. Working on that…

What it did to my immediate family was cause additional stress in the form of:

- My mom having to pay for an attorney on a single-mom-of-two's teacher salary

- Rick tried to convince Kevin it never happened and asked him to talk to me about it (yes he really did that... Kevin was 10ish)

- Me having to go to a therapist to deal with the stress and fear of being interviewed by his attorney and/or it possibly going to court

- The fear and stress of "being deposed"

- Being interviewed by myself, a minor, in a room with only his attorney (and court reporter) who berated and shamed me by saying things like, "You know this never happened. Why are you trying to destroy him?" and "We know you're making this up. You know this isn't true. Why are you lying?"

The lawsuit ultimately went back to the original court, but by the time it arrived there after all the back and forth, I was 18 and I could have legally taken the case on myself as an adult. There is no way in hell I was going to do that, nor could I, even if I wanted to. At 18 I was living in Madison, Wisconsin, attempting to learn "how to college" and live on my own. I was broke. I lived in an efficiency apartment (a single room), just off the Capitol, which meant I shared a kitchen the size of a closet and a bathroom with three other people who had their own single rooms, who I'd never met before.

But... and this is hysterical... you're gonna love this... Rick must have thought that I MIGHT or possibly would take the case on myself, because as soon as I turned 18 he started calling me. Remember, he adopted me when he and my mom married, when I was three. So, technically, I was his daughter.

From the time we left Tennessee and until then he'd never as much as sent me a birthday card or tried to speak to me. He'd never, not once, made an effort to talk to or connect with me in the six years since we left Chattanooga. But, then again, why would he? I was not his daughter and I certainly had no interest in speaking to him if he had made an attempt. Now, however, he was calling me at least once a week to "check up on me."

Once he thought it would be helpful to send me a check for $16.00. When I asked him the following time he called what the money was for, he proudly said, "Well, Christy, it's to help you."

Go on... keep laughing... it's true. Yes, you read that right. He sent me a check for $16. I almost fell off my bed laughing when I saw the check.

I'm not sure what he thought that was going to do for me, or better yet for him, other than appease his guilt. He was a university professor and a politician so I'm pretty sure he could have made at least a little more effort.

Have you ever heard of someone being bought off with $16?

Keep laughing... I'm laughing while I'm writing this because I forgot how ridiculous this was. It's still funny. Pathetic on many levels... but funny.

The trauma drama trial never took place. After years of dealing with this, the financial resources that it depleted, the stress it caused, and the energy that it took, we decided to end it. Mom and I decided to end it for a few reasons.

Her attorneys told us that if it went to court there were only two possible outcomes.

1. **We could lose** – he never had a record or any other criminal complaint against him YET and he was a big dog in academia and politics. I would also be subjected to being on the stand, questioned, and more than likely shamed and discredited in front of a jury. We knew that would end badly for me and I'd already suffered enough in the deposition.

2. **If found guilty** he would go to prison for 10 years. The reality of that for Kevin would be unmeasurable. It would fracture the fabric of our little three unit family and that was not an option. Kevin shouldn't have to suffer more for his father's flaws.

That's the long story, with all its tendrils, of how I told my mom about the abuse.

I was stressed.

I erupted.

She found out.

It affected many, many people, not just me.

The trauma and its drama began...

But wait... there's more.

I want to make a really important point here.

Pay attention.

PLEASE PLEASE PLEASE pay attention.

In this country alone the current statistics of childhood sexual assault as of 2020 are:

- 60,000 children yearly in America are victims of substantiated or indicated sexual abuse

- 55% of assaults are "at or near the victims home"

- 48% were sleeping, or performing another activity at home

This is me. This is also A LOT of other women AND these are also ONLY THOSE WHO REPORTED.

I believe the top main (there are many) reasons that children don't report, or women who were sexually assaulted as children don't report, is this (BECAUSE THIS IS SCIENCE and real life).

When you're a child and shit happens to you, your built-in safety system (autonomic nervous system) takes over for you, to keep you safe because when the assault is happening it is too much to process. Part of your brain goes offline (prefrontal cortex) so you're not entirely aware of what's going on because it's too overwhelming.

The stress chemicals that are swirling around in our bodies while the assault is going, and that more than likely stay there, cause fuzzy thinking, so when asked, we MAY

NOT remember everything crystal clearly. As children we don't have the capacity or words or experience or skills to fight off the predator, so a lot of us go into a freeze or shutdown mode because it is safer than trying to fight or run away.

We've seen and heard time and time again of women speaking their truth about this only to be shamed and blamed and not believed because they were questioned "Why didn't you tell the story earlier?" or "Why did you wait so long to tell anyone?"

Let's chat about this for a minute.

THE SHAME & BLAME GAME

Shaming is hateful and does more harm than good and is typically done by people who do not understand how trauma works. Believe me, I've shamed myself enough. I certainly don't need others to do it, nor does anyone else.

What's that saying? "Unless you've walked a mile in someone's shoes…" paraphrased from the Mary Lathrop poem "Judge Softly," people need to stop. When you judge someone you are telling the world that you know better or you would have done better. Discounting and discrediting the person and or their experience in question is shameful. End of story.

VICTIM BLAMING… No one asks to be assaulted. Especially a child. Regardless of how short a skirt was or any of those other ridiculous phrases you hear being said that negates the victim's experience and puts her at fault.

We also shame ourselves. Consciously or unconsciously we do it. We do it because our maladaptive behaviors that are a result of unprocessed trauma continue to play out in our lives, through being overwhelmed and not understanding why. Through over reacting instead of responding. Through feeling like we are not good enough because the voice of anxiety and depression in our head tells us we are not. Through struggling in personal relationships and not understanding why we keep attracting drama.

I also want to put a new spin on this for a moment. This may not be new to some of you, however it may be the first time a few of you have heard this. Hear me out before you throw this book across the room and it breaks your favorite thing.

If you were assaulted, there's about a 300% chance that your assaulter was victimized too. Just like the line in the song from the musical *South Pacific* that says "You have to be carefully taught" (which is about teaching racism), you also have to be carefully taught, I mean groomed, about sex and how to use it as a weapon.

Ask yourself: "Who assaulted them? Who assaulted the predators?"

And before you get mad about this... hang on... I am NOT letting this person, the predator, off the hook.

I'M NOT! Really. I just want you to look at it from a more global and generational trauma perspective. The big picture, if you will.

Who messed with them? What other lovely, scared, traumatized, stressed, messed up, scared child, post-traumatic, stressed out, angry, sad, adult who hadn't dealt with their own shit, victimized them? And, for that matter, how far back does that really go?

Take a minute to breathe that in…

Do you see where I'm going with this?

The reason I'm bringing this up is because I've spent many hours and years thinking (when I'm not in my victim, sad, depressed, and stressed pity party brain) where did he learn that? Meaning Rick, my abuser.

Who messed with him? Was it someone he was related to? Was it someone he trusted? How old was he? What did they do to him? Where did it happen? Who was supposed to be protecting him? Was it at his house? Was he sleeping?

If you've never thought about this… as my girls say, "sorry not sorry." Exhale. These big aha moments take a minute or year to process.

If you have thought about this… well done! You've stepped back, maybe took a huge pause, exhaled, and looked at how this messy life works from a different perspective. Let's keep growing and learning and raising the frequency of us and our world together.

Please know this is NOT me LETTING HIM OFF THE HOOK.

Oprah said many years ago in an interview (my ears honed in on this like the universe was speaking to me directly, when the guest was explaining how trauma works). Oprah's response was, "We should be asking what happened to you instead of what's wrong with you." Which is now the title of her widely popular book, *What Happened to You.* My perpetrator's behavior, his predatory behavior, is an EXPLANATION not an EXCUSE.

TEACHABLE MOMENT

This looking deeper, bigger, broader is part of my work, and that's part of why I'm writing this book – for all of us to gain perspective. A more global universal perspective of how trauma and healing works. To heal not only myself, but hopefully it prompts you, if you need it and others as well. Trauma work and healing first starts with you. Your intention to heal. Your curiosity about how things work. Your commitment to learn how to love yourself through healing. Understand that not everyone is affected in the same way. Each of us has a nervous system that can respond in a variety of ways to what the universe gives us. Once we understand how trauma works, how our nervous system works we can hopefully be more gentle with ourselves. Give ourselves and others more grace. We can begin to use tools that serve us as we heal. We can heal future generations and co-create a world where we all want to live. Amplify your curiosity which can cultivate more compassion.

Now, it's your turn to decide what to do with this...

Movement Versus Self Medicating

movement

is

freedom

Somewhere in the mid-to-late-1980s, when I was in college for the first time (or "practice college" as I call it, because I discovered partying, drugs, drinking, dancing, and more, and basically majored in "State Street" – a street off the Capitol building in Madison, Wisconsin, with great bars, restaurants, and shops) I also discovered movement. Well, discovered might be the wrong phrase. I like to say it found me, if I'm being honest.

It must have been 1985 because I graduated from high school in 1983. I was in my second year of practice college and I was looking out the window of our apartment on North something Hamilton, a four bedroom just off the capitol that I shared with three roommates. The window in the living room overlooked the street and across the street you could see into the basement window of whatever building was there at the time.

I have no idea what made me stop and look across the street, because I have no memory of ever doing that before. But I remember very clearly staring out the window and realizing that I couldn't move. I was glued in place, watching these women move in weird clothes to music and they were laughing. What was this? These women were moving back and forth, side to side, laughing, having fun, smiling to music. I had no idea what the hell they were doing, but I knew at that moment I needed to do this. Every part of my body needed this.

The Reason We Exercise is Not What You Think

I've been an exercise geek for over 30 years. I really believe it's saved my life… and no, I've never had a plan to end my life. But as someone who has a history of childhood sexual abuse and is a self-employed, single mom, I have a little stress and definitely some trauma which ultimately makes me feel like shit more often than I'd like… unless I do my work daily. The childhood sexual trauma I endured historically made me not feel safe in my own skin. I spent most of my life feeling bad, feeling uncomfortable, feeling "not good enough.

There are those huge moments in life (almost like the universe steps in and says, "pay attention to this… this will be huge for you…") that I vividly remember. Discovering exercise was one of those universal interventions for me.

Seeing those women move, my brain screamed very loudly at me. It said, "I need this!" It looked like fun to me and I always craved fun. Yup, you guessed it, this was the 80s and aerobics was the big new big thing. Big hair, leg warmers, thong leotards, leggings, scrunch socks, and white high top tennis shoes. Well, the thongs came later...

I was hooked. I took my first aerobic class – yes in those bright stretchy leotards and I finally started to feel good or at least better. What was this magic? The key word here is "FEEL." Up until that point I'd spent most of my life often **delightfully dissociated** and in a **functional freeze** (a stress and trauma response to threat), which up until the last few years I'd never heard of. Most of my life I don't remember ever feeling anything but numb or sad, unless I was with my friends or moving my body, which usually made me happy.

Being in a constant freeze meant I couldn't necessarily feel things because my body was chronically in protective mode and dissociated, because being present in a lot of situations felt overwhelming to me. My nervous system was preprogrammed to be on high alert from the sexual assault. It defaulted to the "freeze" state which it went into during the assaults. Meaning my system thought I was in danger and it had to protect me from whatever that danger might be regardless if there was a real threat present or not.

Once my body was introduced to movement and it became a regular ritual, I started to come out of my freeze a little. I began to feel better in general. I engaged more. I got out there more. I lived more. I laughed more. I was able to feel... a little.

I taught Aerobics. I taught Step. I taught Spinning. I taught more... I also walked, ran, biked, worked on the equipment at the gym, and more, almost daily for the next 30 plus years. I did it because I felt better when I did. I don't like feeling bad because I already felt bad more often than not.

What I didn't know until a few years ago was that I was using movement to manage my stress (increased cortisol levels, the stress hormone released into the body to be used as fuel for fight or flight) and keep me sane. I knew when I exercised I felt better. I was calmer. I was clearer headed. When I didn't, I felt bad. Simple as that. When I feel bad, my resilience goes down; my trauma drama brain can take over. Life can be more challenging.

As I said earlier, one of the results of my childhood trauma was that my brain was re-wired – or hijacked – at an early age to be "on" all the time. By "on" I mean on high alert for danger. My internal safety system was in "protection" mode more than it was in "connection" mode and that's not healthy. Our system is meant to be in a flow between the two states not weighted toward one or the other... that takes us out of balance.

I was in a constant state of fight or flight, which is not something you can just turn on and off. It happens automatically. If my stress isn't actively managed, I can get overwhelmed easily. I yell at my children. I react versus respond. Then I feel bad for acting and feeling the way I did. It's a horrible, ugly cycle.

Being "on" all the time is also exhausting. It drains your energy. I used to push myself hard to do, accomplish, or finish things, even when I was so exhausted I could barely walk. So it does have its perks, but my body and health need breaks from being on all the time. Furthermore, in our society, at least here in the United States, we, especially women, are conditioned to go go go, do do do, take care of all the things. But we are not taught to slow down, not to mention take care of ourselves, it's hard to slow down when you're in a constant state of fight or flight unless you actively work at slowing down. Balance is key, but we're not taught that.

I also have anxiety and depression (as do a lot of women with childhood sexual trauma). Most articles and research on childhood trauma relate the correlation between the trauma, how it affects the developing brain and overall health and wellness into adulthood. Research can also identify a potential predictable trajectory for hardship and suffering of children who've been abused, neglected, and more in adulthood. Possibly earlier.

One of the biggest bodies of research that identifies the correlation between early childhood trauma and health is the Center for Disease Control's **Adverse Childhood Experiences Study** (ACEs – often billed as the "Biggest Public Health Study No One Has Ever Heard About"). The study identifies examples of mental health consequences for those who've experienced childhood sexual abuse (and other abuse and neglect) and those include depression and PTSD symptoms. Anxiety and depression are right at the top of "symptoms" for those of us who have sexual abuse in our history.

"The CDC-Kaiser Permanente adverse childhood experiences (ACE) study is one of the largest investigations of childhood abuse and neglect and household challenges and later-life health and well-being. The original ACE study was conducted at Kaiser Permanente from 1995 to 1997 with two waves of data collection. Over 17,000 Health Maintenance Organization members from Southern California receiving physical exams completed confidential surveys regarding their childhood experiences and current health status and behaviors."

Why did exercise help me feel better? For a variety of reasons. Personally, for years exercise was my social connection. We are designed to connect.

* https://www.cdc.gov/violenceprevention/aces/about.html

It was the perfect feel-good. Movement. Music. Laughter. Fun. I was around happy sweating people. It was amazing. The perfect recipe for happiness for me. I loved teaching group fitness classes. It was a win-win on so many levels. I taught people to sweat, laugh, and have fun while increasing their cardio and strength capacity, and, depending on what I was teaching, I got a workout in myself. It was wicked fun.

Don't get me wrong, it was work too... prepping choreography, creating profiles based on real life, prepping playlists, making sure I had daycare. But it was still magic. Regardless of how tired I was before class, or how much I told myself I absolutely didn't want to teach today, I always walked away feeling better physically and had a much clearer head. My mood was also always better. I was more up (emotionally) after class, even if I was in a good mood when I arrived, I always felt better after.

I also loved movement outside and alone. Now, after being a fitness teacher for over 30 plus years and a mom for 20 plus years and a single mom for 17 years, I also crave solitude. My church, for lack of a better term, is my morning personal practice. I walk, I hike, I bike, I yoga, I stretch, I lift, I practice TRE®. And when I'm done and when there's time, I sit and I listen. Or I slow down on my return home if I'm walking or biking and I listen. It's pretty amazing what comes through.

Exercise as medicine is not a new concept, however if you ask anyone who has a movement practice they will more often than not tell you they feel better after. There are countless articles and studies that support my Exercise is Medicine mantra.

In a 2019 Harvard Medical School article addressing exercise as an antidote for anxiety. Author, Dr. John J. Ratey stated, "One in five Americans over 18, and one in three teenagers 13 to 18, reported having a chronic anxiety disorder during the past year."*

How does exercise help ease anxiety?

- Engaging in exercise diverts you from the very thing you are anxious about.

- Moving your body decreases muscle tension, lowering the body's contribution to feeling anxious.

- Getting your heart rate up changes brain chemistry, increasing the availability of important anti-anxiety neurochemicals, including serotonin, gamma aminobutyric acid (GABA), brain-derived neurotrophic factor (BDNF), and endocannabinoids.

- Exercise activates frontal regions of the brain responsible for executive function, which helps control the amygdala, our reacting system to real or imagined threats to our survival.

- Exercising regularly builds up resources that bolster resilience against stormy emotions.

* https://www.health.harvard.edu/blog/can-exercise-help-treat-anxiety-2019102418096

Using exercise as medicine in the mental health field is also becoming a supported method for managing symptoms. I have issue with the word "problems" but the 2019 article *Exercise is the New Primary Prescription for Those with Mental Health Problems* by neurosciencenews. com, which sites a 12 month study with 100 participants in a mental health facility, is particularly encouraging.

"When it comes to inpatient treatment of a range of mental health and mood disorders – from anxiety and depression to schizophrenia, suicidality and acute psychotic episodes – a new study advocates for exercise, rather than psychotropic medications, as the primary prescription and method of intervention. Findings from the study reveal that physical exercise is so effective at alleviating patient symptoms that it could reduce patients' time admitted to acute facilities and reliance on psychotropic medications."**

With mental health fast becoming a global crisis, we need all the help we can get. I'm certain we can all agree that medication is not the solution for everything. For some depression and anxiety, it is a bandaid to manage symptoms. But in most situations, it does not get us to the root cause of the issue that is causing us grief.

So yes, it is about movement. But it's also about being still. There has to be a balance. If not, we're fostering the perpetual fight or flight state in which a lot of us live.

** https://neurosciencenews.com/

When I do my work (body-based/somatic) I feel better. When I don't, I can and often do feel bad. I don't like feeling bad. It's exhausting. It doesn't mean I will, but I can, and it does happen. My depression is an interesting beast and has a personality of her own. I think of it as the dark side of wellness. My depression has its place. I believe it's trying to teach me to rest. My body needs deep rest and I've never taken the time it needs to rest. How could I when I've been in a constant state of "running," as one of my teachers told me? When she made this statement, I assumed she meant physically and I laughed because I've always wanted to be a runner. I did for a while and then my body said, "girl, you are not a runner, calm down."

What my teacher meant was that my system was always "running in the background." She was referring to my nervous system being in a constant state of "running," not me literally. It took me a while to understand that. What I've learned over the last few years is that my depression has its place and for years has been trying to tell me to rest. To listen. To slow down. That there's some shit (emotions) that needs to be addressed. The more I stay busy the more I deny that I have shit to deal with. The more I act like everything is ok when it's not, the louder she gets. The more I deny that she's there, the louder she gets. The more I shame myself for having depression, the quieter she gets. Because shame is what we do with emotions we have or states we are in that we don't understand or society labels as bad.

So I acknowledge her. She's part of me. If I deny this part, I'm denying part of me and that's not healthy. It took me a long time to accept that I had depression because of the social conditioning.

There are many, many people I know and love who have depression and many with a formal diagnosis. I've never judged or thought less of them, but when it came to myself I did judge. Weird. I was very judgy about myself.

Plus I'm certain I was hiding and masking my depression with exercise and maybe too much wine or other fun things.

When I finally acknowledged that I had depression and that it was ok, that it didn't make me any less, I decided to not only listen but to try and turn it on its head and make it fun.

I gave her an identity. I picture her as having the badassery of Bellatrix from *Harry Potter* and a force that commands the attention of Medusa. Dark. Mysterious. Scary at times. Beautiful. Powerful. Exhausted from all the badassery work.

Well, it works for me. Because when she shows up, I really don't care for it or feel like I don't have time to be depressed because there are too many other things I need to be doing. But, as I said, she serves a purpose. She makes me slow down.

I need both movement and rest. Happy and sad. I appreciate both. I need both to appreciate the other. That's what wholeness is about. Loving all of our parts. Trauma separates us from ourselves. So the work we need to do to heal needs to focus on bringing us back together. To wholeness.

Our society is so scared of the whole idea of a "mental health diagnosis." We're scared of anything that we don't understand. So what do we do? We either ignore it or act like it's not there. We shame and blame it. We medicate it. We hide it. We keep it in the shadows and somehow think that's healthy. Look where it's got us now.

Side note: On my birthday (very interesting...) in May of 2020 I received an email (a report) from the United Nations, "Policy Brief: COVID-19 and the Need for Action on Mental Health." I think it's ridiculous that we had to wait for COVID to come around before there was a global look at mental health, but that's just me. It noted:

> Before COVID-19 emerged, statistics on mental health conditions (including neurological and substance use disorders, suicide risk, and associated psychosocial and intellectual disabilities) were already stark: The global economy loses more than U.S. $ 1 trillion per year due to depression and anxiety.

I don't have a formal diagnosis of depression. But I've had many conversations with my people (friends, family, colleagues, doctors) and they all agree, "why and how would I not have depression?" It runs in my family and then there's the assault and more. And life. A few years ago I tried taking meds for it. My depression amps up in the winter, especially around February. The meds did nothing for me.

IMPORTANT:
I am NOT suggesting that people should not take medications for depression. I am saying it didn't work for me, for my flavor of depression anyway. It does work for some people in my family. Just not me. I have mild to moderate depression. Moderate more in the winter months.

The point I'm making here is that exercise helps with anxiety and depression. There is hard data that identifies the correlation between exercise and mental health and using exercise as a stress management tool. Yes, stress and mental health are related in my world. They are close, personal friends.

If you take just a few minutes to dive into Googleland and look up the benefits of exercise on mental health, you'll see articles from the National Institute for Mental Health, The American Psychological Association, The National Institute of Health, and The American Council on Exercise, to name a few.

The sited benefits include:

- increases the "feel good" hormones and neurotransmitters
- rewires the stress response
- improves self esteem
- sharpens memory
- reduces PTSD symptoms and depressive symptoms

"Exercise strengthens our memory and makes us sharper, happier, and more resilient (a very popular word in wellness right now). Studies show that vigorous exercise is a better antidepressant than Prozac."
-Dr. Mark Hyman

It gets better. A 2022 article in *The New York Times,* "The Healing Power of Strength Training," identifies a former military officer who harnessed the power of strength training to help him feel safe and give him a sense of agency and self control. The article also shared a story of a mother of two who was diagnosed with C-PTSD (chronic PTSD) and how weight lifting helped her "feel safe, calm, and grounded outside the gym." It also discusses how "working with resistance" helps build resilience.

Until recently I didn't focus a lot of energy on weight lifting/strength training (huge cardio freak here), although I've known for years that as I got older I would need to for nothing other than the added calcium benefit. However, when I do lift, whether that's working with body weight training or light lifting free weights or using resistance machines, I always feel mentally stronger. The relationship is pretty amazing. When I feel strong in my body, I feel stronger emotionally.

I can't count the number of times I've felt weak in my life. Whether it be physically or emotionally. When the assaults were taking place, I couldn't fight back, I couldn't stop what was happening to me; the message that was sent to my system was that I was weak.

When I was a child and this was happening to me, I didn't have the conscious thought, "I'm weak." I never heard that in my head or told myself that. It was unconscious and always lying just under the surface of my skin, a constant hum or an emotional foundation might be a more accurate description. This foundation implied "you're weak, not good enough, not smart enough, not loveable enough." I never actually looked in the mirror and said those things to myself; it was a knowing, a felt sense deep in my bones.

The one thing I did for most of my life, prior to my late 20s, that might be construed as saying those things to myself, was a habit that developed when I looked in the mirror. As soon as I saw my reflection, I would shake my head no. Almost as if I was subconsciously saying to myself, "you suck."

As I got older, and was at a different place in my life, with a solid movement practice, this habit started to die down. I became aware that I was doing it. I started asking myself why I was doing that, where did this come from, and then I eventually stopped.

The negative self-talk can be emotionally debilitating. The other nonverbal ways it showed up in my life were a broken record of "I'm not smart enough," "I'm not good enough," "I'm not pretty enough," "I'm too tall," "My hair is too curly," "What's wrong with me?," "My thighs are too big," and on and on and on.

So... back to weight lifting... There is a direct correlation for me between weight lifting now and how I feel mentally as an adult versus how I felt as a child when I felt weak. I think of it as paying myself backwards (like paying it forward). I'm healing and strengthening this body now which still carries the memories and emotions of the past.

I want to close this section by speaking directly to you if you are a mom with this history or are a mom of someone who is.

There are three main reasons (albeit there are about a million more...) we have to do this work in this body now.

First and foremost, we have to break the cycle of generational trauma and to do so we need to heal. Healing trauma requires us to address the emotions stuck in our bodies and heal in a way that brings us back to wholeness.

Second, we are not taught how to take care of ourselves on an emotional level. Meaning deep delicious practices that ultimately bring us back to wholeness.

Third, we unintentionally share our shit (unprocessed trauma) with our children. That furthers the cycle.

The first one I've already addressed and will discuss more later.

The second, when I say we are not taught to take care of ourselves. What I mean by that is really taking care of ourselves. Not just the maintenance of being a human (brushing teeth, showering, clipping toenails) I mean having a movement practice that our body likes. I mean learning to recognize and sit with uncomfortable emotions. I mean having regular play and fun. I mean eating foods that are good for us. The list is long.

Lastly, unintentionally passing our shit on to our children is supported by science. We know we pass on genetic traits. Eye color, height, and other physical attributes, which are easy to see. We also know that some of our children have inherited our anxiety. Our depression. Our health issues. However, we also pass on our emotional baggage if it's not healed. This is specifically important as a mom to understand due to a term in the mental health and trauma fields known as **"neuroception"** or "detection without awareness." It's how our nervous system evaluates risk.

Understanding the theory of neuroception as a parent is paramount. Why? Because it tells us that we as humans neurocept off one another. It means that we unconsciously send signals and pick up signals from one another through our autonomic nervous system or our "personal surveillance system." Our automatic nervous system is our built-in safety system, always scanning our environment for cues of safety. Always asking: Is this safe? Am I safe? Is this person safe?

The term neuroception comes from a body of research by Dr. Stephen Porges, *The Polyvagal Theory.* Dr. Porges, a distinguished University Scientist at Indiana University, is the founding director of the Traumatic Stress Research Consortium. He is Professor of Psychiatry at the University of North Carolina and Professor Emeritus at both the University of Illinois at Chicago and the University of Maryland. I've been fortunate to attend a few of his presentations related to TRE® (tension and trauma releasing exercises) training and a Polyvagal Institute training.*

Deb Dana, one of Dr. Porges' colleague, explains neuroception like this… "Neuroception describes how the nervous system takes in information below the level of our **conscious awareness** via three pathways: inside our body, outside our body, and in-between our body systems."**

Meaning our internal state coupled with our external experience and the communication between those two are translated as our detection without awareness. It happens automatically without us knowing and therefore affects everyone around us… subconsciously.

* https://www.stephenporges.com/about
** https://www.pacesconnection.com/topic/new-episode-of-transforming-trauma-the-rhythm-of-regulation-exploring-the-polyvagal-theory-with-deb-dana

Look at it this way… think of yourself as a cell tower. You're always sending (and receiving) signals from those around you. It's part of your being. It just happens. You do it without knowing that you do. AND those around you pick up on your signals as well, though we are not aware of this on a conscious level. It happens without our awareness.

This is why we as moms (parents, actually anyone) need to do our work. Here is the body of research that identifies that we emit our stuff subconsciously to those around us. My favorite example of this is how my girls have endured my anxiety through my hypervigilance to keep them safe and always supporting them to the best of my ability. Historically when my anxiety was high, my girls could feel it. They could sense it. Their systems could sense it even when they were little and didn't have a sense of knowing what it was. My anxiety and my depression had a direct impact on them. It wasn't a conscious thing on my part to share this, but it happens. My anxiety influenced them. We pick up on each other's energy and emotions often without knowing that it's happening.

My anxiety. My anger. My fear. My everything is shared with them. Then their system has to figure out what to do with it. Over time this has an impact on those around us. This is why taking care of ourselves with self care practices that feed us, caring for our emotional health, practicing self regulation, and ultimately doing repair work if we need to, breaks the cycle.

> *"A neuroception of safety is necessary*
> *before social engagement behaviors can occur.*
> *Infants, young children, and adults need appropriate*
> *social engagement strategies in order to form*
> *positive attachments and social bonds."*
> ~ Institute of Educational Sciences (ERIC)*

I did not sexually assault my daughters, yet they still were the recipient of the mess I was carrying in my body and will continue to carry on this journey. Just like I inherited and then shared all of my mother's unresolved issues. She inherited and then shared all of her mother's unresolved issues. Imagine how far back this goes?

Sharing with each other isn't only limited to the sad and unhappy obviously. It's also the fun, the happy, the joy. However, when we have unresolved trauma in our bodies, some of us default to the negative so it's critical that we actively work to heal and part of healing is to feel. If we are in a frozen state (I believe my family has a very long history of being in a frozen state), feeling can take effort. We have to feel the sad, the hurt, the angry, but we also have to work at the happy, the fun, the joy.

Think of the impact this could have on your family. It will affect your family in the now, but it will also affect generations to come. If we as women all collectively did our work, healed our old shit, now, we could potentially

* https://eric.ed.gov/?id=EJ938225

mitigate some of the pain, suffering, and yuck for our future daughters, granddaughters, great-granddaughters, great-great-granddaughters and on... we could heal the world. It's worth trying, don't you think?

I do want to acknowledge that "exercise" is not always a positive option or even an option for some. Life happens to all of us and with everything, it's contextual. There are those of us who have addictive tendencies and do too much and those of us who can't exercise due to other circumstances. I get that.

Well... here's the deal with that. I believe everyone needs to have a movement practice. Balance is the key. Balance in life is everything. So if you have addictive tendencies, practice balancing it with yoga or some other practice that requires you to slow down. Find what works best for you that brings you back to wholeness.

If "traditional exercise" is not an option for you due to other life circumstances, then find a movement practice that does work for you that makes you feel good. There is always something out there... get curious to see what options are available. Exercise is one of the many tools I use to help manage my anxiety, depression, and stress, think clearer and **feel** better and I am so very grateful for that one day back in Madison when the universe said "stop, look, pay attention."

Education and an awareness of how things work is a win as well.

TEACHABLE MOMENT

Healing work requires effort and does not happen overnight. Nor should it. We all can do this work. Whether you are doing it for yourself, your daughter, your granddaughter or your own mother or grandmother. Any work we do in this body on this planet in this lifetime heals generations front, back, left, and right. We simply need the intention to do it, the right tools, and time. "The Intention to Pay Attention" is key. Stay curious, have the intention to heal, and set a course of action to do the work.

What I want you to know is that the science behind healing trauma is growing. We know so much more now than we did even a year ago. We also know that those of us with childhood sexual trauma are predisposed to anxiety, depression, and a myriad of other lovely things. Exercise is an evidence-based proven way to help mitigate (manage) the effects of anxiety and depression. Start moving. Do it with a friend. Make it fun.

References

"Exercise Intensity Influences Prefrontal Cortex Oxygenation during Cognitive Testing." Moriarty T, Bourbeau K, Bellovary B, Zuhl MN. *Behavioral Science* (Basel). 2019 Jul 26;9(8):83. doi: 10.3390/bs9080083. PMID: 31357450; PMCID: PMC6721405.

How Exercise Can Boost Mental Health in Young Adults
https://www.acefitness.org/resources/everyone/blog/7947/how-exercise-can-boost-mental-health-in-young-adults/

Working out boosts brain health
https://www.apa.org/topics/exercise-fitness/stress

CDC's Fast Facts: Preventing Child Sexual Abuse
https://www.cdc.gov/violenceprevention/childsexualabuse/fastfact.html

The Healing Power of Strength Training
https://www.nytimes.com/2022/07/07/well/move/weight-lifting-ptsd-trauma.html

Exercise as a First-Line Treatment for Depression
https://www.psychologytoday.com/us/blog/the-healthy-journey/202206/exercise-first-line-treatment-depression

Exercise Prompts

 If exercising is not your *forté* then do it with a *friend*

 Go for a *walk*

 Go for a *run*

 Go for a *hike*

 Do something in *nature* that gets your heart *pumping*

 Go *dancing*, *roller skating*, anything that sounds like *fun* AND gets you *moving* and *sweating*

 Join a *local gym* and try a group *fitness class*

 Try a local boutique studio that offers *exercise classes*

 See what's online that looks like fun try: www.bodygroove.com

Laughter & Connecting

laughter

heals

the heart

I don't remember in my 20s having a felt sense or knowing that Laughter is Medicine, however I vividly remember the first time I intuitively used it that way.

My first first huge breakup is when I realized the impact laughter had on me. I was 20 something. It was the end of a four-year relationship with my first love that started when I was in high school. He was a few grades above me. We weren't in a relationship in high school, we slept together a few times and for me that was powerful. I adored him. He was handsome, his confidence was very sexy, and he was popular. In high school I was a wallflower who was trying to figure out how to live in a new town with a very different culture than I'd spent growing up in. I always felt like I never fit in.

How I went from happy, functioning, and involved in everything at school to a wallflower in this new land is very telling for how my system responded to change.

How and why we ended up in Wisconsin is interesting. I'd grown up in the south in Chattanooga, Tennessee. The move to the North from the South was horrible for me at best. Teenage me would refer to it as "being made to move from a school/place where I was popular, had a ton of friends, was a cheerleader, sat on committees, was on Homecoming Court with the Football Quarterback, was first chair flute in the band... so my mom could get away from her ex-husband and be closer to family, relocation plan." Adult me sees this in a completely different light.

The move was very traumatic for me, however, the reason behind it was necessary for my mother. She did what she had to do to survive. She needed to get away from Rick (her soon-to-be-ex-husband and my brother's father) and be closer to family for her sanity. She had been planning to reconcile with him... until the following morning.

The next morning after she agreed to rekindle their relationship, we found him in bed with one of his students. He was a Professor in the Political Science Department at the local University. By "we," I mean my mother, my brother, and I. It was a Sunday morning after church. My mother suggested we go to his apartment to ask him to come over for lunch. One of us knocked on the door and walked into the apartment. My mother called out to him. I noticed a pair of women's shoes on the floor by the door. I quietly pointed them out to my mom. In a heartbeat Rick appeared at the balcony looking down at us (it was a split level apartment with a metal winding staircase to the loft bedroom on the second floor). Realizing that my mom and I'd seen the shoes, he began to back pedal. He was begging and pleading with my mom, "Carolyn, don't come up here, please, it's not what you think." Right! Uh huh…

I followed her upstairs. One of his students, a blonde white girl, was standing in his bathroom with nothing on but a white tee that barely covered her ass. The girl was clearly caught off guard and embarrassed, grabbed her clothes, and ran out. He tried to talk to her at the same time he was trying to convince my mom "it was nothing." I was watching him like a hawk and I'm fairly certain he could pick up on my glaring eyes trying to sear him in half – as any teenager who was assaulted by him and now had a sense that he was also hurting her mother would do.

Full disclosure, I couldn't fully grasp the depth of what was going on; I was 13. What I did understand, at some deep level of knowing, was that he was hurting my mom because she was screaming at him and directing my brother and me to "go downstairs" and then we left.

Shortly after that we packed up her car and we moved from Tennessee to Wisconsin. It happened so fast I don't know what happened. I have no memory of packing my things, loading a car, saying goodbye to neighbors or friends. We just left and drove two days to Minnesota to stay with my grandparents so my mom could figure shit out. What a nightmare that must have been for her.

The three of us in a car, boxes and possibly a kitten or two. We'd done this trip many times before, because both mom and Rick were from the same small town in Minnesota. I was also born there. It was a long two-day car ride and the one good thing about being in a car for two days that made it tolerable for me was that we always stopped at Stucky's restaurant. I loved their pecan log rolls. Still do!

Many more things happened as part of that mad dash from the South to the North. While we were living with my grandparents in the interim, police showed up with paperwork and tried to take my brother back to Tennessee because Rick wanted him back. I remember my mom screaming for my grandma then falling to the floor as she continued to scream, "they're gonna take him, Mom, they're gonna take my baby." I'm pretty sure there's more to this story...

Some time after that and more than likely a ridiculous amount of stress and drama for my mother, we moved to Wisconsin and lived with my Aunt and Uncle on a short term basis until Mom could find a job and we could afford a place to live. Aunt Sandra and Uncle Rich... two of my favorite beings.

When I describe them to friends and colleagues who don't know them, I hear myself say, they are amazing people who used to live in Eau Claire, Wisconsin. They both worked at the University before they retired and moved across the state to Door County. She was a nurse and taught in the nursing program, has survived cancer more than once, is one of the best cooks I know, and has the biggest heart. My uncle worked in the tech department, helped pioneer Distance Learning at the University, has completed more Birkebeiner Ski Races than most mere mortals, and is an amazing sailor and boatsman. They were amazing hosts to the three of us who just showed up with a car full of our things in transition to a new life.

Shortly after we moved in with them, a lovely human broke into our car and stole a lot of our things. I can remember a few things of mine that were stolen, which obviously added fuel to the stress of moving. Not to mention all the other things... looking for a house to live in, finding a new school, and on and on. It was not a fun time. I hated it. I wanted to be back in the South with my friends at my school, where I was popular, where I had friends, and where I wasn't afraid to get involved or connect with people.

What I know now is that on an emotional level I began to shut down. I felt numb. I was disconnected from everything I knew and felt very alone. I was also in a bit of culture shock. I have memories of driving around the new town with my mom and brother looking at houses and saying to my mom, "Why is everyone white?" I have no idea what she said, I just remember having the feeling of how weird it was to me that (at least at that time) I saw no people of color.

Once I started school the differences stood out. I remember the first day of school. It was ninth grade. All the students were standing in the gym and we were being assigned to home rooms. I'm fairly certain I was on a sensory overload at the time but had no idea that's what was happening to me. It was sooooo loud. There were a lot of people. I was miserable, anxious, and probably scared, if truth be told.

I knew no one. Not even the few kids I'd met at the "tour for new kids" were around to talk to. There were so many people. It was a sea of bodies or at least it felt like it to my little stressed out Southern girl self, with the "different hair."

The other reason I was miserable is that I didn't look like any of the kids there, which fostered the alone feeling. I didn't blend. I felt like I stood out like that proverbial sore thumb. I dressed differently. I looked different. My hair is dark curly, and that day it was in cornrows. I had on a red shirt, jeans, and a necklace I really liked that was a gift. It felt to me as if most of the kids, not all, had blonde hair and dressed like each other. I could see and hear hushed comments being made about my necklace and my hair.

One of my first school memories was being bullied about my hair by at least one boy. Let's call him Bill. I was clearly sensitive about my hair because in this new land no one had hair like me... It was another instance when I felt like I didn't fit in anymore, like I had in the south. Standing out and being visibly different was the last thing I wanted at age 13. I just wanted to hide.

The hair bullying story is important because teens can be mean as we all know. I was on the bus on the way home from middle school and sitting close to the front. I'm certain I sat there so I could get off fast and go hide in my room again as fast as I could. Bill was sitting directly behind me. He started calling me Rosie as in Gilda Radner's character on *Saturday Night Live*, Roseanne Roseannadanna, over and over and over again. I asked him to stop. He didn't. I continued to ask him to stop. He didn't. The bus driver also did nothing. I finally turned around and clocked him in the face. I was probably as shocked as he was. I'd never hit anyone... ever!

Don't get me wrong... I love Gilda. I've read her book. I love her characters and probably cried when she died, but making fun of my hair in reference to the character's hair (which was made as a gag and shaped like a massive curly triangle) was just way too much for me at that time. I couldn't handle it. So I reacted by lashing out. It wasn't something I consciously decided to do. It just happened. He never teased or bullied me again.

As for my hair... I love my hair now, but I didn't always. My mother never knew what to do with my hair other than keep it short or put it in braids. I am white for all purposes or at least on all of the standard forms in the U.S. My family background is Greek, German, Danish, and Swiss, and I have dark, curly, sometimes frizzy hair (in some circles I'm the white girl with the black hair). When I have a tan (I love the sun) and my hair is doing its thing, I can look mixed. So I definitely didn't blend in this new city of white.

Not blending, not wanting to make the move, to leave my friends, to give up all the things I participated in at school, and leave my neighborhood friends, had a huge impact on me. It was too much for me and as a result I emotionally shut down.

I basically retreated into myself. Instead of being involved in everything at school, I did nothing. I ended up last chair in the band, did nothing extra, and spent a lot of time in my room watching TV (**numbing**)... as was my coping mechanism in Tennessee when I needed to escape or didn't have plans with friends. Instead of connecting with anyone, I went into protection mode by hiding.

I craved my old life where I was popular and I felt like it had been taken away from me. Even if I hated Rick and what he did to me, it was still my life and it was a good life for me at 13.

In Wisconsin, I felt like I didn't fit in and it felt like no one liked me because I didn't fit in to any of the clicks.

In Tennessee I don't remember there being any clicks. Everyone had friends. My lack of self esteem and confidence due to all the newness coupled with an overloaded nervous system from the assault that was still living in my body was a bad combination for me.

My self esteem was the biggest thing affected by the move. I went from a relatively happy and connected kid to feeling like shit all day, every day. I was sad (what I now know to be depression), I felt like I couldn't function, and I had no interest in getting involved or doing any of the things I'd done as a teen in school as I had before. I went on auto pilot (an emotional freeze) and only did what I had to, to get by.

I did make some friends, one of whom I'm still close with today. Jenny. We met that first day of ninth grade and have had our heart strings connected ever since. We've been through hell and back, we were college roommates in Madison, Wisconsin, in each other's weddings, survived divorces together, survived raising children together, traveled to Greece together countless times, cried, laughed, hugged and I love her dearly. To this day she is still one of my biggest cheerleaders, or champions as my uncle puts it. We all need champions.

What I now know was that I was overwhelmed with newness and my already taxed nervous system didn't feel safe. It went into a freeze state as it had done during the assaults. This time however, it was an emotional freeze not a neurophysiological (brain and body) one. My body did not freeze to protect itself as it had then, it was my emotional state that went into a freeze because it was overwhelmed.

This frozen emotional state affected me academically and socially for most of my years in high school and most of my memories of those years are fuzzy at best. I have a few snapshot-like (vague) memories: being in Marketing Education and competing in "Districts," working to create the new DECA store and a few other things the DECA students did, being last flute chair in band (which always made me feel like shit coming from being first chair, but I did nothing to change it), falling on the ice walking home from school and ending up with stitches in my lip, smoking my first cigarette with my friend Jenny in the woods by her house, going to a Go Go Girls concert with a group of girls who I'd always wanted to like me and getting so drunk on the way there I threw up before the concert. Not a lot of specific memories for a four year span.

The overall sense for me then was that I felt bad all the time.

However, in retrospect, I was one of the popular kids in my school in Tennessee and so maybe I was unaware of how other kids felt who didn't feel like they fit in… now that's a thought… turning the tables. I just have no memory of everyone in the south being so divided at school.

72

This doesn't mean there weren't any, it just means if there were, I have no memory of this. I don't remember kids being divided up by sports or smoking or how they dressed or who they hung out with. It seemed to me that everyone in this new school knew everyone else. That they'd all grown up together (mostly) and if you didn't look a certain way or weren't blonde, or a cheerleader, or you smoked, or or or... you didn't fit in. This is how I felt. My reality. I obviously can't speak to how it was for others. Not fitting in, not really connecting, was a horrible feeling.

However, as I look back on it now, I'm certain that it couldn't have been as bad as I remember. It was how my nervous system was responding to the situation. I was always hiding. I always had this deep sense (not feeling... there's a difference) that I came across as a scared little kid and so unsure of myself that why would anyone like me. It's a horrible cycle of self deprecating thoughts which then can actually become a reality. The unintended self-fulfilling prophecy here is lousy for anyone, but when you combine being a young girl in a new school, new city, hormones, regular school stressors, and just plain life (not to mention trauma), it's enough to overload even the strongest of us.

The sense of feeling unsafe and fearful was always there, lying just a few layers under my skin. Sometimes it was more prevalent than others. But it was always there.

The takeaway from the "how I became a wallflower" (the mad dash to the north) is that it was too much for me to handle given what had happened to me prior. It was, however, necessary for my mom. She did what she had to do to keep her sanity. She instantly became a single mom again, in a new town, and more. The responsibilities and the newness for her must have been overwhelming. I'm grateful she had her brother and sister-in-law to buffer the change.

I know she had no idea how much I was suffering internally. I may have told her, I may not have. Thinking back though she must have known or sensed something because she was always giving me "positivity" books. The ones with positive quotes designed to help change the negative thoughts that are always in the undertow.

I know I wasn't even aware of how much it affected me until much later when the proverbial shit hit the fan when the sexual assault story came out (my tipping point). Had we known then what we know now about trauma and how it affects us, my "shutting down" may have been different. There may have been support for me in some fashion other than watching endless hours of TV and drinking with friends.

The importance of the story of the move and how it affected me had a direct correlation to the change in my thoughts, feelings, and actions about myself. It changed me from an engaged and connected kid to one who disconnected from the world but who also craved attention.

So... back to my first love... I fell for this person and then after some time we developed into a relationship where I felt loved. I felt wanted. I felt connected to someone. The relationship with him, although it didn't develop into a relationship until years after we met, was the first time I really allowed myself to feel without being guarded. Feeling had been a scary place for many years and really only happened when I'd had a few drinks and could let my guard down.

We met when I was in high school and he was a few years older. I thought he was magic. He was a hockey player. Watching him skate on the ice took my breath away. He could glide, weave, spin, almost dance on the ice as if he were flying, slide sideways to a stop and make it look effortless. That movement with grace, speed, power, and ease was something I'd never seen up close and I was in awe of him.

And everyone around him looked up to him like he was a god. Or so I thought. He was definitely a force in my life and I adored him. He was this force and I was a wallflower...

During the first few years we were in the same physical space often because I made sure I could be there to be near him. He barely noticed me in the beginning. I wasn't one of the guys and as much as I desperately wanted his attention and to participate in the conversations I couldn't. I had absolutely no confidence in myself.

He was the big brother in this group of boys who'd grown up together. I became friends with the group as did my friend Jenny. Once he noticed me and I let him know how I felt, we slept together a few times, but there was no relationship, just messing around. I always wanted more. He never did. Of course there was drinking which encouraged the "messing around" because, well, it's Wisconsin.

A few years passed. I graduated from high school. I moved to Madison to go to practice college and then moved home again. Somehow, I don't remember how, but we reconnected. One thing led to another and we ended up moving in together. I was absolutely a different person. I'd been to college. I'd lived on my own. I'd partied with the best of them. I'd dated. I'd lived. I had a degree.

I also didn't fawn over him like I did in high school. I'd gained confidence in myself those years of living on my own and going to school. Self confidence is sexy and when I was in high school and we were in the same space I oozed lack of confidence. That may have been the trick, ha. Upping my game by going to school. Interesting how the universe works.

There is something to be said for making that scary leap and moving away to college. (Hint... if I can get through college in a high functioning frozen state, you can, too). Who knows... but somehow this time was different and we were in a relationship. We ended up living together for almost five years. I helped raise his daughter. My family loved him. His mom hated me. We had fun. A lot of fun. A lot of it involved drinking... surprise!

We split up once for a short while after I found out he'd been spending time with someone else. I found notes in his car that she'd written confessing her love for him. I was a wreck. He moved out for a while. I was working retail at the time. I sold women's high end business and casual clothes at the mall during the day and coped with my grief by sitting in our apartment in the kitchen alone at night, drinking massive amounts of wine, smoking a lot of cigarettes, not eating, crying, and numbing out. I don't remember how we reconciled or how long the separation lasted. We reconciled, he apologized, and we lived together for a few more years. I loved him. First loves are rough.

The saving grace for me initially during this break up was the exercise. I was religious with aerobics because it kept me sane during the day when I was not working. I always felt better during the class and when I was done, although the feeling was short lived.

I made new friends during this time, which he didn't feel comfortable around. Towards the end of the relationship, I ultimately went back to college with the intention of being a good and more mature student so I could have a life and a career. I began my undergrad in Marketing Education. I was going to be a teacher. It runs in the family so it made sense and I really enjoyed Marketing.

Over the years, though, I realized just how different we really were. I tried. I loved him. But when I went back to school, things really fell apart and our differences were highlighted. By differences I mean we came from two very different backgrounds and didn't have any similar interests other than music. He liked softball, racing, playing pool, and drinking. I liked movement, music, and dancing, and although I hadn't developed or spent time learning what I did like beyond that, I knew I didn't like the things he did. I simply went along for the ride because he liked those things.

Ultimately his drinking became an issue and he spent more and more time away from home with "other" friends as I continued to grow with my new friends and my college career.

The pivotal point of the beginning of the end was during the second semester of my first year back in school. As part of a Lit class we were reading a short story about two people in a relationship who were growing but not growing together (I wish I could remember the story). It hit me like a lightning bolt. I felt like the story was about us and my favorite professor had chosen this just for me. I somehow knew it was ending for good this time.

Hint hint... another example of universal intervention. Ultimately we split for good. This time it was hell. I moved out. I left him, his daughter, and our little family. We agreed that we'd stay in touch and maybe "work things out." We also agreed that I would continue to spend time with and be able to see his daughter who I'd raised and loved deeply.

With this break up, I was still a wreck, but this time I had other things to occupy my brain. Work. College. Teaching fitness classes and working out on my own. By this time I'd started teaching aerobics, had the best new friends (who would ultimately become more like family... yes, you Sue, Lisa, Andrea, Chris, and Stacy), and am confident that it was the exercise that kept me sane... during the day.

Nights and weekends were rough. And when I was alone, I felt like hell. The grief and the loss of us, his daughter, our life, was the worst. I'd never felt like this before. Not even when we'd split up for those few days years before. This was a different type of pain because I wasn't numbing out with wine. This was heavy. This was depression. My depression never shows up when I'm with people or when I'm exercising. It shows up when I'm alone. It waits.

My saving grace was the exercise and being with my friends. I was finally connected to something. I had found my tribe. I was part of something. When I taught aerobics, I felt better. When I was with them... my new friends... I felt great. We laughed, we ate, we sweated together, we'd dance our asses off together at the clubs, we'd dress up for Halloween parties, and we had formal holiday meals together. It was magic. It really was. I'd never felt so good, felt so a part of things, they were my tribe and I loved them and am grateful for the years we were a family.

However, the good feelings from being around my new tribe and the exercise wouldn't last forever. When I was alone, the depression would return. I still relied on TV to numb out at night... just as I had when I was little and felt alone... there's nothing wrong with TV... it was the amount of TV I was watching.

Interestingly enough, just as the universe had intervened back in Madison when I was dumbstruck watching those ladies exercise, and the story from Lit class, the same thing happened once when I was watching *Saturday Night Live*. Robin Williams was hosting. I loved to watch him work and laughed so hard my stomach and face hurt. I love that kind of deep laughter.

This is the important thing! I started to notice I felt better after laughing. And I was alone when this happened. It was amazing. I never felt good when I was alone.

I'll say that again. Pay attention.

I started to FEEL BETTER after laughing. This was huge. I came up with a plan to try my own laughter therapy (not sure if that was a thing back then). I thought I was brilliant and had made up a new thing. Ha! Well for me it was new... It was like the universe stepped in and said, "Here, this works. Do this!" So I did. And I laughed and laughed and laughed my ass off.

I rented every single Robin Williams VCR tape I could get my hands on just so I could laugh. I also watched as much of *Saturday Night Live* as I could.

Robin did a set on Tammy Fay Baker (former TV evangelist's wife who made big headlines for a variety of reasons that I'm not going to give time to here). Robin was bouncing around the stage in his usual fashion. He did this thing with his hands and referred to her hair as the "Jiffy pop hairdo." OMG. I thought I was gonna pee, I laughed so hard. I may have... The result? I felt amazing for hours after that and I continued to watch things at night when I was alone that would make me laugh.

Laughing was magic for my depression. I'd found another tool that was helpful and I could access it any time I wanted. Laughter and exercise, I now had two tools that helped me feel better and the feeling better started to last longer this time.

I'm grateful to Robin that his comedic work impacted my life so deeply. He was a brilliant comedian. I am also grateful that his life story helps bring depression and mental health into the spotlight. I'm sad that he is no longer with us on this planet, but he absolutely lives on and continues to bring laughter and joy to people who watch his work.

Those of us carrying around trauma in our bodies and who have depression need more laughter and joy in our lives. We need to work at finding those things because our system can default to the unhappy and sad pretty easily.

Around the time of his death it was very publicized that he suffered from severe depression. Robin died by suicide in 2014 at 63 years old. He had been diagnosed

81

with Parkinson's disease, and an autopsy showed he had Lewy body dementia.

Dave Itzkoff, the author of *Robin*, the story of Robin Williams, was interviewed on CBS. The interviewer asked him, "When we're grappling with his death, almost four years later, what stands out to people, what do you think?"

His response was, "Well, I think it's hard sometimes for people to reconcile this idea that somebody who either was so joyful or who made it their purpose to bring a lot of joy to other people, could be suffering privately behind the scenes..."*

What I find fascinating about this interview is that he is spot on about "people suffering behind the scenes." We all suffer. We all mask. Some of us do it in the dark. Some of us do it in the light. But we all suffer to some degree or another. It's part of the human experience. I've been aware of this with myself and others in my life, but to hear it about another who brought so much global joy to the planet made me really think about this idea, which was a surprise to me, too. Comedians are "on" on stage. It's a performance. It's not life, the behind the scenes life we all live.

Which is the prompt for the next thing... we, as a society, choose to view the suffering, the sadness, the depression, the trauma as if it doesn't happen. That is the issue here. We, at least here in the U.S., act as if "it doesn't happen." By that I mean we ignore it because it makes us

* https://www.cbsnews.com/news/robin-williams-mental-health-zak-son/

uncomfortable and we don't like to be uncomfortable. I'm very grateful for the celebrities who have come out publicly to disclose their depression. This is what we need to normalize it. This brings connection. We need connection.

We agree on things like 9/11 and Hurricane Katrina and we accept those national traumas. We all read or hear about the stories of paedophilia and sexual predators when it comes out either from a religious organization or in Hollywood. But it shouldn't have to be an over-the-top scandal that affects large numbers of people or a horrific tragedy to bring it to light.

Hell, it should be part of mainstream conversation. Not taboo just because it makes us uncomfortable. We typically shy away from things we don't understand or that make us uncomfortable. Which leads to fear. Fear stops everything. Having those hard conversations is where it starts. Having real conversations. Learning about depression. Learning about mental health. Learning about how trauma works and affects us, especially for those with Adverse Childhood Experiences is a conversation we as a country need to be mainstream to take out the stigma and stop the shame and blame.

I believe that one of the positive outcomes of COVID is that it's brought mental health to the forefront of humanity. I hope that conversation continues. I hope it sheds light on it and makes having a diagnosis, or having someone you love have a diagnosis, less taboo. Having these conversations brings awareness which can bring connection.

Discovering the positive impact deep, rich, delicious laughter had on my mental state was very big for me. It helped me feel better longer, so I made it an actionable part of my life.

As time went on, I didn't have to search for feeling better through laughter as much as I did then. It came more naturally (especially when I was exercising and laughing together... that was the magic).

I say "search for" here because I have a ton of vague memories from my life of people telling me to smile. Which to me implies that I was either looking too serious or checking out (dissociating)? I have no idea, but clearly my affect was not a happy one or so I'm inferring here. Which in reality was how I felt on the inside most of my life.

Inside I was not happy. Maybe not "not happy" more like numb, empty, no feeling at all. Frozen.

What I've left out here is the profound impact this had on me academically. Before the move I was a great student with good grades; I graduated at the bottom of my class in High School because I was in survival mode more often than not.

Imagine the implications this has on the world of education when we understand how it works and systems are readjusted to fit current reality.

HOW WE LOOK ON THE OUTSIDE/MASKING

your inner reality
creates your
outer form

For a lot of us, how we present ourselves in this world is often different than how we feel on the inside. For some of us being "on" all the time can be exhausting. For a good portion of my life I think I presented on the outside like I was ok, while on the inside I was either a wreck or numb. I masked very well and really thought I was doing a good job of it until it was brought to my attention. This was made very clear to me at a continuing education conference for Spinning that I was at in Chicago in 2002. The World Sports and Spinning Conference (WSSC), where hundreds of instructors, trainers, and the founder Johnny G were spending time together.

This again is one of those times that I remember with intense details which is hysterical because the overall conference I was so overloaded that I barely remember anything. But this two-hour training session is glued in my memory. I was in a session with one of the Master Spinning Instructors. The session title was "The Dao of Spinning." I loved this and was eating up every piece of content he had to say in the theory part of the session.

When done with the theory part we were instructed to "move your bike to any location in the room, facing any direction, and just ride. Also, to listen to the music with our eyes closed and do whatever feels right."

I remember thinking… *Really? Just ride? With no instructions or coaching or or or? Hmmm. Ok.* So we did. I and all the other Spinning Instructors in the room moved our bikes. He started the music and got on his bike that was on rollers (his outside bike was on an indoor trainer that uses cylinders to simulate the road and challenges the rider to be more mindful among other things). I was so impressed. He made it look effortless. I had a hard time keeping my eyes closed. What I really wanted to do was watch him ride hands free (his hands were in a namaste/prayer position at his heart) with his eyes closed while riding on these rollers. It was sooooo cool to watch. But I was a good student and wanted to comply (people pleaser).

As we were riding he caught me watching him. Our eyes met and he smiled. Then, without words, he urged me to close my eyes and smile. It was like he saw right through me. I was so uncertain of myself and what to do without being told. I was overwhelmed. My anxiety was high because I felt like I had to be "just so." I was surrounded by hundreds of fitness professionals from around the world and I felt like such a phony. Even though I'd been clinically trained and certified with the organization, had taught for many years, and taken hours of continuing education. I still wasn't good enough to be there with all the other talented people. Trauma brain...

I took his advice, closed my eyes, and really got into the ride based on what felt right with the music, its beat (cadence for pedaling), and a natural rhythm for my upper body to engage in. I got lost in it. I smiled. And then... I cried. Not sobbed. Just cried. The kind where tears roll down your face but you can still see and if you wipe them fast enough no one will notice.

The combination of those things music, movement, and closing my eyes so I could "tune in" to me... was the magic. It connected me to me.

A lot of us with Adverse Childhood Experiences live in a perpetual cycle of stress and fight, flight, freeze, flood, or dissociation. When you are in those states, more often than not, having an internal awareness (**interoception**) can be next to impossible. Interoception is a sense that allows you to feel sensations from inside your body. For example, interoception allows us to know if we are feeling hungry, full, or nauseous.

It was the combination of the movement, the music, and tuning in that allowed me to connect to that buried space of fear. I realized I was crying because I was carrying a lot of fear and anxiety in my body about the next big thing coming up in my life. It was my brother's wedding and I was part of the wedding party, so was my daughter, *and* my brother's father: the man who molested me. The fear and anxiety was buried so deep that it took the music, the movement, and tuning in (closing my eyes to block out the visuals of the room) to bring it up. I was embarrassed that I was crying in public, plus it surprised me that this fear and anxiety about being in the same space with Rick was still there and that it was buried deep in my body. I thought I was over that... well I was wrong.

Given the exercise and the laughter, the college degrees, and my amazing group of friends who I felt were family and who I trusted and spent many many hours, days, nights, and weekends with, I thought I was golden. I was happy. I was connected. I was healed. I thought I had it together because I was feeling better more often than not. So I was shocked when this fear and anxiety about seeing Rick surfaced. I thought it had just gone away.

There was only one other time in my life that I had to be in the same proximity as him... when my brother graduated from high school.

That was different from this because the gradution was held at a huge arena. He did not sit with my family and the only opportunity to be in close proximity to him was outside (much safer than inside) the building after the ceremony was over where we'd gathered to congratulate my brother. It was a brief moment being in the same airspace as he was in, however I remember feeling shaky and anxious. I made certain he could not see it because I was on high alert to see where he was at all times.

The one thing that stands out, and I vividly remember as he walked up to our little group, is that I could feel his eyes on me. I immediately turned my back to him. I remember thinking he couldn't get to me (emotionally) if my back was turned, sort of like an energetic f--- you. It was summer and hot and I had on a beautiful green backless dress I loved, however the moment I realized I'd be in the same space he was in, it made me feel vulnerable and exposed. When he appeared I turned around. I desperately wished the dress was not backless because I felt even more exposed and as if he was staring right through me. It was very creepy.

The rub here and why this is important... This was the first time I remember having any physical emotion about his father. By physical emotion, I mean a conscious thought that had a feeling attached to it. I'd spent most of my life in my head about it. Avoiding it basically and or with little to no feeling. Maybe anger. Yeah, probably anger...

I was nervous about the wedding because I didn't know how things would go. Another way to say that is I knew I couldn't control the situation. My two-year-old daughter was also going to be in the same close quarters with him, so I was nervous and a deep subconscious part of me knew that I needed to be on high alert to protect her. She was the flower girl and part of the ceremony. I knew everyone there, well almost everyone there, regardless of whether they believed me or not, was aware of the assault and that there was a story.

THE WEDDING STORY

A quick recap of the event. The wedding was beautiful. I was always very aware of where he was at any given moment. I avoided him at all costs. I'm pretty sure I dissociated for most of the day, because I don't remember most of the event, only snapshot memories as with other big events in my life. What I remember was my hypervigilance to stay away from him and to keep him away from my daughter.

The reception was another story. It was lovely. It was also more difficult to steer clear of him because unlike the wedding where it's more organized and people are at times "in their place," the reception is more of a free-for-all with the exception of the meal.

See my control issues coming out here? Yup there they are... my internal safety alarms were on high alert and my fight or flight was ready to go at any given moment. So I needed to control my environment. My autonomic nervous system was doing its job to keep me safe because I didn't feel safe around him.

The momma bear in me was also on high alert and in protective mode. I knew I had to keep him away from her. I think I told everyone in my inner circle (my mom and her best friend) to keep an eye out for him being near her if I was dancing or they were in charge of her.

There was one point later in the evening when he did approach me in the hallway, just outside of the reception room. I felt pretty certain he was drunk. My memory is fuzzy here (that's one thing my stress hormones did for me, they blurred my thinking so I could act and not take too much time to think in the event I needed to run). I was either holding her or with someone who was holding her in the hall.

He came over, stated how nice it was to see me. I froze. I think. Meaning I physically froze. He asked if this was my daughter and proceeded to ask if he could hold her. I almost ripped his face off. The internal rage I sensed was like a volcano about to erupt. Was he serious? There was no way in hell I would EVER let him near her, not to mention "hold her."

I'm pretty certain I told him there was no way he'd ever hold her or get anywhere near her. I might have said why and other things. I'm not sure. The next thing I remember was him leaving, walking out the door to go outside, and I went back into the reception feeling very shaky. I of course had a drink or three to calm down.

Being in such close proximity and having him speak to me directly triggered fear. My body didn't feel scared. I don't remember my body feeling anything other than shaky and anxious. I remember just knowing. It was a sense. Not something I said to myself. It just was. I also sensed that I had to be "on guard" all the time and I blamed myself for being selfish because it was supposed to be a magical time for my brother. I remember thinking that I was a selfish asshole because this was his magical day and I was quietly making it about me... at least in my head I was.

The reason this is important is that regardless of how long ago the assaults took place, my body still remembered the fear. It was visceral. I'd been to therapy to work through it. However my body was clearly holding onto the memories, the fear, so it responded appropriately. My alarm system was triggered and I was ready to fight or flight, not freeze or fawn as I did when I was a child with him during the assaults.

Regardless of all the work I'd done to feel better, to be happy, my body was still holding on to fear and the emotions of the experience. I was often happy on the outside but still empty or frozen on the inside. It's hard to be happy, joyful, playful, and peaceful when you can't feel the insides of your body. Laughter, however, did help me connect with my insides when I was able to get to that deep delicious belly laughter. The connection between laughing and the body is visceral.

I know I'm not the first one to discover the benefits of laughter as medicine. I started researching laughter as a health benefit. What I found was amazingly more than I first anticipated. I'd known about Laughter Yoga for years and seen the Patch Adams movie that details how laughter heals.

One of the original thought leaders of laughter as medicine was Norman Cousins. After being diagnosed with a debilitating illness he took his health into his own hands and with his doctor combated the illness with a combination of laughter and vitamin C. He wrote *Anatomy*

Of An Illness after he reversed his disease with this regime. Cousins was a longtime editor of the Saturday Review, global peacemaker, a political journalist, a professor of medical humanities at UCLA, and a recipient of hundreds of awards including the UN Peace Medal and nearly 50 honorary doctorate degrees. He is famous for saying...

"I made the joyous discovery that 10 minutes of genuine belly laughter had an anesthetic effect and would give me at least two hours of pain-free sleep."*

and

"Laughter serves as a blocking agent. Like a bullet - proof vest, it may help protect you against the ravages of negative emotions that can assault you in disease."*

I recently took a Laughter Wellness Workshop. It was so fun! Highly recommend it. Why did I take a Laughter Wellness Workshop?

- I thought it would be fun.
- I was looking for more tangible evidence on the benefits of laughter.
- I'm working on adding more fun and play in to my life (necessary for healing).

* https://health.mountsinai.org/blog/medical-clowning-is-good-medicine

According to Sebastian Gentry, the workshop leader and founder of Laughter Online University (LOU), "Laughter is a big part of the solution," for life's challenges. Sebastian is a French-American laughter and wellness expert with a passion for emotional literacy. He has appeared in 100+ newspapers and magazines and two TEDx talks, as well as major TV shows, including the *Oprah Winfrey Show*, *60 Minutes*, and ABC's *Good Morning America*.

Gentry not only researches, studies, and teaches laughter wellness, he practices it as well. In his article, *Science of Laughter*, he shares a list of tangible benefits that include:** (these are just a few)

1. Exercises the diaphragm, regulates Blood Pressure, reduces pain and increases oxygen.

2. Laughter is the #1 natural enemy of bad stress because they are physiological opposites.

3. Increases the immune system's defenses and improves natural defenses against illness.

4. Helps to naturally create a healthy DOSE of wellbeing (dopamine, oxytocin, serotonin, endorphins).

5. Reduces stress, anxiety, tension, and counteracts depression symptoms.

6. Elevates pain threshold and tolerance.

7. Improves interpersonal interaction, relationships, attraction, and closeness.

** https://www.laughteronlineuniversity.com/benefits-of-laughter/

My own personal favorite Laughter as Medicine story happened just a few years ago. Remember the famous scene from *When Harry Met Sally*? It's got one of the best non-sex sex scenes I've ever seen. It is brilliant.

I bring this scene from the movie up because one of my favorite people in the world, Carleen, and I had a *When Harry Met Sally* moment at a Panera restaurant a few years ago. Today if I think about that lunch I still get the endorphin rush and smile like the Cheshire Cat you'd think it happened yesterday. I can still feel the fun living in my body, and that feels amazing!

We were catching up on life in general. It didn't involve sex, well, we were discussing my sex life, however I wasn't faking orgasm like in the movie. But we were laughing so hard I'm pretty sure I peed a little. No, I know I did. We'd just come from a session with a mutual friend of ours who did some work with us and we were going over what we'd discussed with our friend.

By the way, during the session with our "friend"
I was told that I'd write a book, a memoir about my life.
I laughed and said, "who the hell would want to read
about my life?" ...thanks Lisa

95

One thing led to another and we started laughing. I mean big, loud, massive laughing. The kind that starts slow like a water washing up on the shore and then turns into a crashing of waves. We laughed, we paused, we laughed louder, we paused, we laughed harder, we paused, and on and on and on. We couldn't stop. I kept saying, "We're gonna get kicked out of here," and we'd laugh harder.

Panera was packed that day. We were obviously making a scene. People walked by with their trays and smiled. Some gave us a weird look and some nodded with approval. Some laughed with us, just more contained.

The best part? When a woman from a few tables away said, "I don't know what you two ordered, but I want that." Then she came over, introduced herself, and said how we looked like we were having so much fun and to keep it up. We smiled, agreed, thanked her, and kept laughing. I have no idea if we actually ate any food. I remember my stomach hurting for days.

My point here is that laughter is magic and helps us feel so good. And clearly the feel good lingers in our bodies just like the feel bad does. Whether it's spontaneous, stomach aching, losing-bladder-function laughter, or something you actively seek out like watching your favorite comedian, laughter heals and it's also contagious.

Remember what I said before that a few people laughed with us? I know when we left Panera that day, we shared our happy with others simply by allowing the raw unfiltered laughter to happen. It oozed through the restaurant and I also know that people, like trees, have unseen communication systems, which means they felt the joy we were feeling. Call it energy, neuroception, or magic, whenever you're near someone laughing, jump in, and ride that joy wave with them.

I believe that we need to find more ways to laugh, to play, and to have fun. We are not meant to be "on" all the time. We are (at least as females in the U.S.) taught to go go go, do do do, be be be, and take care of others. That's too much pressure. That's too much work. It unbalances us. It's stressful and if you add trauma and other shit to it, well that's enough to put any one of us into overload. And overload is a dangerous place to be if you're a mom, if you own a business, and are expected and/or needed to show up for others for whatever reason. You will crash… guaranteed, if you don't take time for yourself. Take time to play. Take time to laugh.

Coming from an educational background I appreciate data, social proof, and evidence-based validation. You may have heard of some of the following… enjoy.

*"Laughter is the tonic,
the relief, the surcease for pain."*
Charlie Chaplin

*"Laugh often, long, and loud.
Laugh until you gasp for breath."*
George Carlin

*"Laughter serves as a blocking agent.
Like a bulletproof vest, it may help protect you
against the ravages of negative emotions
that can assault you in disease."*
Norman Cousins

*"Your body cannot heal without play.
Your mind cannot heal without laughter.
Your soul cannot heal without joy."*
Catherine Ripperger Fenwick

*"Laughter is the sun that drives winter
from the human face."*
Victor Hugo

TEACHABLE MOMENT

We are designed to connect and laughter heals. Stress and burnout are on the rise, especially for women… because not only do we make all the people (thanks Trevor Noah for that reminder), but we take care of all of the people. It's time to flip that paradigm on its head and take care of ourselves, or at a minimum simultaneously while taking care of others, first. By taking care of ourselves we help mitigate the negative affects our shit has on those we love. Whether you need to heal trauma, develop a daily personal practice of stress management and self care, or just feel better for a minute… you have to take the time for you. Yes, just like the oxygen mask theory…

I laughed so hard tears ran down my leg

"Given the brain's neuroplasticity, it's to our benefit to make our lifetime experiences as positive and hilarious as possible."
Psychiatric Times, 2019, Kavita Khajuria, MD

Neuroplasticity is the brain's ability to retrain itself. It's the science behind the "you can teach an old dog new tricks." The brain is adaptable like plastic. Neuroplasticity, also referred to as brain plasticity, is a term used to describe changes to the brain that happen throughout the lifespan in response to new experiences. Ultimately the more you do something, the easier it is to do it again. We can retrain our brain to be happy! So laugh more, smile more, look for things that make you happy, bring you joy, and make you laugh. Brilliant!

Ways to increase your laughter and fun

 Watch your favorite comedian OR Go see a comedian live

 Put on your favorite jam, lock the door and bust a move

 Put on a clown nose... see what happens... seriously

 Play the staring game with someone

 Hang out with someone who makes you LAUGH

 Watch "Whose Line is it Anyway" OR Get involved in Improv

 What else can you think of?

I'm sharing this list of some of my favorite female comedians in support and gratitude. Love them!
Lucille Ball, Gilda Radner, Carol Burnett, Wanda Sykes, Tina Fey, Ali Wong, Tig Notaro, Taylor Tomlinson, Michelle Wolf, Eliza Schlesinger, Sarah Millican, Hannah Gatsby...
(this list is truly endless)

The Fall Out of Always Being "On"

As women we do all the things. We are urged, suggested, invited, directed, shamed, and historically and culturally coded to do all the things. This means pushing through. If we don't push through, shit falls apart. Or so we think. I've lived this, watched my mom live it, and heard this from my students and clients for years.

I grew up watching my mom rarely ever sit down unless she was grading papers or doing some other "paperwork" thing. She was always busy.

As women, we multitask like nobody's business. We have multiple jobs. We have multiple professional degrees. We make all the people. We take care of all the people. We have side gigs. We are thought leaders. We are change agents. We solve the world's problems while driving (or in my grandmother's case, in the middle of the night when she couldn't sleep). We clean, shop for, and change diapers, cook, workout, and have an encyclopedic knowledge of our house, our childrens' things, their school things, their friends, their friends' parents, including what they do, and on and on and on...

This physical and mental multitasking has a horrific long term effect on our systems. It's not good for us and it's also not efficient. I can't tell you how many times I've found my full coffee mug in the linen closet or on top of the dryer. Or gotten in the car and then had to go back in the house more than once to grab what I needed, like... maybe keys or my favorite water bottle or even my daughter.

We're also raised in a society that negates our emotional well being. Our emotional health. Our mental wellness (a new phrase that I love). We cannot do "all the things" and simultaneously take care of ourselves. There are not enough hours in a day, not to mention a week to get everything done and try to be healthy in a very unhealthy world. That is unless we loosen the reins and re-train ourselves to take care of us first.

I have no memories of my mother taking care of herself shy of the basics (showering, teeth, etc.). I'm chalking that up to a few things: single mom of two, professional, academic, working for a cause, never witnessed her mom taking care of herself. I have no idea how far back in my family this goes. She also helped take care of my grandparents and my great aunt and uncle when they were at the age they needed help. She had a lot on her plate all the time.

The only down or play time I remember her being involved in was watching TV, roller skating with her best friend, or occasionally going out to dinner. She was probably too exhausted to try to figure out how to have fun.

We also are raised in a society that fosters individuality as opposed to community, which is the opposite of how we were designed. We are designed to connect. Other cultures are designed to support one another. We are raised with phrases that foster this go go go attitude that doesn't allow us to truly take care and heal when we need and or do it in a collective manner which isolates us even more.

"Put on our big girl panties."

"Don't cry."

"It's not that big a deal."

"You can do it."

"That happened a long time ago."

"Why can't you let that go?"

I'm sure you've heard most if not all of these phrases and probably have some gems yourself.

These platitudes are so common in our culture that, as women, I'm pretty sure we started to nod and smile generations ago when we, in our higher thinking brain thought, "Wait a minute, that can't be right." But since society has always supported these patterns, we just kept going like the Energizer Bunny. We just kept going without taking a moment to see if it was the best thing for us or not. Or to take time to process what just happened. We live on momentum instead of living in the moment.

We are amazing. But, at a certain point, too much gets to be too much and if we don't take care, our system will take care of us. Our nervous system will take over and make us think, feel, and act in ways we may not be so proud of later, or, better yet, we may not understand because we are out of balance.

This, I believe, is how my system told me, "Girl, I am done."

The years before, during, and immediately after my oldest was born, were wicked stressful. Some good stress, but still, wicked stressful.

What follows are some stories from my lived experience that show as example how this has worked in my life.

A Different Kind of Stress

Sometime in the mid 90s I met my first husband. We actually met online before online dating was a thing. We met when the internet was new and I was researching how to use it for a college prep course I was preparing to teach to high school students. I was also going to Greece with my mother for the first time to see the amazing place where she met my father. So on my lunch break, I'd look up sites on Greece. Just to tell you how new the internet was then, there were three sites, YES THREE, about Greece. I found a guest book. I wrote something. He wrote back. History happened.

He lived in Greece and I flew there often. I loved being there. I'd never met my Greek father so going to Greece was new for me then and he knew everything about the country. It was magic. I felt like I was in a fairy tale. I loved the food. I loved the islands. I loved the warm sun. I loved the sea. I loved a lot of things about Greece.

Among the things I didn't love was the ridiculous traffic. The smells from the exhaust while stuck in stop-and-go traffic in the 100 plus degree heat. That I didn't understand what anyone was saying (the first few times) even though I attempted to learn a little of the language. I didn't love the ad posters that replicated at least a dozen times in a row every few feet (mainly for cigarettes and cellulite removal) and I hated the graffiti. My system easily was overwhelmed on a sensory level even though I loved being there.

Fast forward after a few years of international dating, many trips to Greece and meeting my father's family, he proposed at Christmas while with my family. When he proposed it was the second time in my life when I was speechless. Literally. The only other time I was speechless was when I met my father for the first time. (We are a family of talkers… so speechlessness is not our norm.)

I accepted his proposal. Getting him here to the states after he proposed was a miracle on its own, and this was pre-9/11. The paperwork. The wedding planning while he was still in Greece, because he could only come here two weeks before we were to be married, on a fiancé Visa.

Our first wedding was in Greece, and on the return trip I got pregnant with our first daughter, Maya (I have two stunningly beautiful and talented daughters, Maya and Melina).

Our second wedding was here in the States. Family, friends, food, dancing, etc. You're familiar with U.S. weddings. The one in Greece, though, was a whole different story. If you've seen *My Big Fat Greek Wedding* by Nia Vardalos... well, it is sort of like that, but without her amazing writing and built-in humor. It was magical.

I was dressed with the help of many... as in the movie, and had my makeup and hair done by all the women – my soon-to-be mother-in-law and sister-in-law, her best friend, and her sister, and possibly a few more. I was primped. I was polished. I was adorned with jewelry. It felt like it took hours.

My amazing soon-to-be mother-in-law had outdone herself with the planning for the details that were needed to pull off a wedding and had also planned a spectacular and stunning reception for after the wedding.

The wedding itself is blurry to me because it was filled with many traditions I wasn't familiar with. Wearing matching crowns on our heads that were connected together with a ribbon called *stefanas*, walking around a baptismal font, kneeling and kissing the hand/ring of the best man... yes, you read that right. AND NO I was not a fan of that, even though he was wicked handsome. He was also Maya's *Nonos* (godfather).

After the ceremony was over it was even more of a blur. We stood with the other people in the wedding party to shake hands and be congratulated, similar to what we do in the states. The big difference was the money and tiny envelopes of money people would literally and almost aggressively shove in our hands and pockets. This sea of people all had a look of love, joy, and congratulations on their face and I was in shock.

I remember seeing people reaching over tops of other people and pushing to get to us to give us this magical gift of money. It was amazing and I am very grateful for the gifts, but I was not prepared for the sea of people coming at us all at once. I liken it to when I've seen a celebrity being loved on by fans and the fans try to get close and touch the celebrity or give them gifts. It felt like that to me. It was meant out of love and excitement, however, not having ever seen or been near this massive outpouring of joy I was overwhelmed.

The reception was something out of a fairy tale. It was at an outside venue in downtown Athens with beautiful lights everywhere. I felt like royalty when we entered the venue and were greeted with applause. We entered. We ate the most amazing food. The cake was to die for. We danced. We laughed. Sadly, the venue Dafne was destroyed in the 1999 earthquake and I'm not sure what happened after that.

On the way home to the States, we stopped at my new husband's friend's house in New Jersey. This is where I got pregnant... and yes if you're wondering if the friend knew that's where I got pregnant, she does. She is my youngest daughter's *Nona* (godmother) and we joke about that room and that bed.

I was shocked when I learned I was pregnant. I'd been told by a few doctors over the years that I'd probably never get pregnant because the endometriosis I'd had when I was younger was bad enough that, "parts might not work" so well due to the damage my insides had gone through… I had a laparoscopy (scope and scraping out my insides) to "handle" the crippling pain I'd get monthly. I was ultimately told that yes it would happen again. The surgery was not a one and done.

Maya's Birth

The year after I gave birth to my oldest, Maya (named after Dr. Maya Angelou, one of my heroes), my life turned inside out, to put it mildly.

As weird as it sounds I don't remember feeling fear much in my life. Which is really an odd thing to even hear myself think. I remember feeling bad a lot, although I was never able to put a name on it or label it. I don't remember feeling fear. The first time I actually remember feeling fear, no let's call it terror, was when I was giving birth to Maya.

I was sick almost the entire pregnancy. Yes! It was soooo fun! I used to hate those women who'd say, "I loved being pregnant; it was magical..." or whatever adverb they'd use to describe the longest year of my life. Seriously? They must be nuts. Who would love this?

I had migraines, nausea, and (stress) food cravings oh my! I ate horribly. I craved and then proceeded to eat French fries, Pepperidge Farm Chocolate cakes, ham and cheese sandwiches (which I'd get up in the middle of the night and eat with a glass of chocolate milk; can you say hello diabetes?), watermelon, corn, chocolate shakes, and patty melts. I couldn't exercise, which had been my magical stress management system and lifeline for years. I gained 75 pounds. I missed my friends and was miserable.

I'm pretty sure depression was part of the mix as well, but I had no idea that's what it was.

> Side Note:
> I don't remember depression being a subject that was talked about anywhere in my life before, with the exception of one night when my mother couldn't get out of bed. I had no idea what was going on and it was odd. I remember questioning what was happening. My grandparents were there to help out. It was never discussed.

Food Stress

I really did crave ham and cheese on white bread (the kind that shouldn't be sold as food). I'd wake up in the middle of the night starving and eat. My poor body. My poor, poor little baby. I wish I could say that if I knew the damage that those foods were doing to us together as a collective unit, that I would have chosen to not eat them, but I'd be lying.

As bad as I felt all of those months, I gave into any food that made me feel better in the moment. As I said, I gained 75 pounds.

Time skip – during my second pregnancy I started to learn about our food systems in this country. I had time to read so I took advantage of it. My food journey started with reading Barbara Kingsolver's book, *Animal, Vegetable, Miracle* which led to learning about The Weston Price Foundation, The Slow Food Movement, Gut and Psychology Syndrome, and much much more. I took an avid interest in eating healthy, whole foods and made a point of understanding where our food comes from, who grows it, and, yes, who funds the growing of it. I also joined a local CSA (community supported agriculture) and helped with the growing and tending to the food we were eating.

Just because I was an exercise freak for many years, doesn't necessarily mean I was a healthy food geek. Before I had my second daughter, Melina, I ate whatever I wanted and disregarded how I felt after I ate or wasn't able to correlate the two.

Towards the end of the eighth month, I developed toxemia. My mother was staying with us by now and I was put on bed rest and was told that if this list of things started to happen (face and or feet began to swell) that I had to go to the hospital immediately. I was on bed rest for exactly one day and then was admitted because my face swelled up like a balloon. We called the doctor and were told to "come now."

We grabbed my already packed bag and headed for the hospital. They admitted me immediately and were told that they would watch me overnight. If nothing happened on its own, I would be induced in the morning. They would "encourage the baby to come" if our bodies couldn't figure it out together.

The next few hours were a blur and then it was evening. I was going to be induced. They were going to "encourage" the baby to come earlier because of the toxemia.

I was hooked up to machines and spent the night contracting.

I watched *My Cousin Vinny* because it was the one movie my dad and I watched together before he died and it made me laugh. I knew laughter was a medicine for me.

I was given only one of the two sleeping pills prescribed because my nurse had just returned from vacation and hadn't followed or misunderstood her orders because she was tired. I overheard this from my medical team.

The 10-12 hours of severe cramping off and on was a nightmare. I was in and out of the shower all night, blasting water from the shower head onto my stomach to ease the pain. It worked... for a while.

Sometime around eight the next morning, I was getting prepped for an epidural. I was told they were going to induce due to the current circumstances and they needed to get me "ready."

The next 10-20 minutes felt like time moved at high speed.

I was told to sit up with my legs over the side of the bed and to hold on to the tray table while they put a needle in, next to, on top of... whatever... my spine. They told me why they needed to do this, but all I could think of was, "What if I have another contraction while they're putting the needle in, or what if I flinch or move because of it and then the needle goes in the wrong spot. I'll be paralyzed." Yes, I might be a little dramatic. But the fear was real. I was terrified. See what stress and no sleep does to a brain?!

Fortunately the epidural went fine. But wait, there's more. The next minute, my former college roommate called. After talking for just a minute, my water broke. We ended the call. Then it gets really fun. They laid me down. The machine next to me began beeping.

I then heard my nurse call out loud, very very loud, "I need help in here." Her yelling and the urgency in her voice made me nervous. A small team of people came in. Things started to get real fuzzy. My hearing was fuzzy. My vision became blurry.

My doctor appeared over me. All I could see was his head in a sort of fuzzy, almost glowing way (pretty certain I was headed towards passing out). He then told me what was going on. It didn't register. But what he said next absolutely registered.

He said, "If we don't do this, you and your baby may die. Do I have your permission?" I must have said yes, because the next thing I remember was the team transferring me to a gurney. They ran me down the hall so fast I remember the gurney bumping into walls and before I knew it we ended up in a surgical bay.

The last thing I remember before waking up was looking up onto the ceiling and seeing bright lights as they told me what they were going to do, having my arms stretched out like a T and held down, and me telling them not to start yet because I was still awake… that I could still feel things.

Clearly at some level I understood what they were going to do, but only a little. However it did register that they were going to *cut me open*.

Somewhere between 12-24 hours after the surgery, I woke up and I had a daughter. She was in the arms of my mom's best friend Amy, and I felt like I'd been hit by a truck. I don't remember seeing Maya much due to her being in an incubator in another room and I could barely keep my eyes open, not to mention trying to nurse.

The next few days were a blur. Being in the hospital. The drive home. Being at home with a newborn. Being in so much pain in my stomach that I couldn't sit, lie down, or anything without feeling like I was going to die and then trying to nurse this new being that had just been taken out of my body.

Plus, my stunningly adorable new baby decided she wasn't going to eat. My mother tells me (this seems more like a dream than my reality) that she remembers staying up with my daughter and feeding her with an eyedropper while she lay on the dining room table. The nurses gave us instructions... "She needs to eat or she will die."

Good God! Talk about planting fear. I absolutely know my medical team was doing the best they could, and I am grateful... but that was the second time within a few days that I/we were told we could die.

Was I stressed? Hmmmm... maybe a little.

Recovering from a major surgery without any after care. Not sleeping because my daughter cried as newborns do, and some postpartum depression setting in. Although I didn't know that's what it was at the time.

Plus we (my new family and I... my daughter and my husband) were slated to move back to my home town within a month.

Fast forward. We did move. We moved into the house next to my mother's. My husband was on board with this because this is how he grew up in Greece – living with his immediate family. There were three generations in the same home (with separate apartments) when we first met.

I finished grad school.

I kept working.

Being a new mom. It was beyond hard. It sucked... well part of it did.

Sleepless nights. Screaming. Not eating. Not latching (because breast is best – I was told and I agree). But not at the detriment to the mother's mental health when the baby doesn't latch after trying for weeks at a time and trying all the things to make it work, including multiple consultations with the lactation consultant, a plastic fake nipple – because apparently mine weren't good enough or the wrong size or whatever – pumping in between so the "milk didn't dry up" or so I didn't get an infection, which I ultimately did. Yes, that was fun... and then, to top it off, developing an infection in my breast that made it red, swollen, painful, and hard... oh, it was so fun. The warm compresses I was told to use felt like heaven then when everything else felt so hard.

Who knows these things? It was an up and down roller coaster of God I love this little being more so much I could eat her up and what the hell have I just done? I can't do this...

Depression &
My Mental Health

And the depression that hit, although I didn't know it was depression at the time... now that sucked. It made me question everything including my sanity and life in general. I had really dark thoughts...

"Maybe I'll just leave and never come back."

"Driving off a cliff might be good."

"She'd be better off without me."

And a few other lovely thoughts that I'm even embarrassed to say here... ugh.

I'm pretty sure I had a mild to moderate version of postpartum depression after talking to a friend of mine who admitted she hated parenting and hated life and hated, well, everything since giving birth. She shared more with me, but that's her story to tell. Hearing her story of how bad it was for her, how much shame she had, and how scary...

meaning she thought she was losing her mind (so did I, but was too scared and ashamed to say anything to anyone) validated that I was not alone and no, I was not losing my mind.

Listening to my friend tell me her story made me feel less like an asshole who couldn't handle being a new mom. It was powerful medicine for me.

Hearing other women's stories is valuable. They make us feel less alone.

The following year I got the weight off. I began exercising again, my daughter ultimately learned to eat and sleep (but only when with us in bed – another "no no" told to me by many including my doctors... I call BS). I finished grad school, and life went on.

When Dysfunction Turns into Disease

To say I was stressed as a new mom during the first year after Maya was born would be a gross exaggeration. I was massively stressed, and depressed. One month after her birth, we moved from Minneapolis back to Wisconsin in the house next door to my mother so I could be closer to her for support and help. No stress there... new baby, moving, recovering from surgery, and nursing. I should have taken a cue from my cat Sam who was so stressed with all the newness, that he had to take anxiety meds.

I tried to nurse for almost a year. It failed miserably. I tried everything, including working with the lactation consultants, using the nipple extensions (plastic things to make my nipples fit in her mouth easier, what a nightmare). I was still recovering from the emergency C-section and still uncomfortable in my body with the extra weight that I couldn't lose. I was miserable.

Maya always had a hard time sleeping and needed to be rocked to sleep or sleep on me or her dad. When she was put down in her bassinet or crib she screamed. Those were the days when pediatricians told me to "let her cry it out, she needs to learn to fall asleep on her own." She would scream and I would sit on the floor outside her room and cry. I hated thinking the doctors knew best (they did go to medical school) and I was wrong to want to hold her until she stopped crying.

Even though my gut instinct was to hold her. My body ached knowing she was suffering and I was told to just let her suffer. I put my trust in the doctors instead of listening to my inner wisdom.

Needless to say, sleep was not an option for us back then, unless I let her sleep on my chest or next to me and then I felt guilty because I was going against the doctor's orders. If I only knew how damaging that was for her… We place too much trust on others when we don't trust ourselves.

That entire first year was a blurry nightmare! Little to no sleep, her father working what seemed 24/7, I cooked, cleaned, mommed, and more. On top of momming a newborn, I'd also kept my graduate assistant position at UW-Stout, continued to work on completing grad school and was teaching Spinning a few times each week.

Just as things were beginning to calm down, or so I thought, very weird things started to happen. My hair started falling out. The room would start to spin and my heart would race for no reason. I was light headed often and dizzy. I also began to lose weight. I had no idea what was going on and I thought I was losing my mind.

A few times I'd get so dizzy that I would have to grab on to the kitchen counter so I wouldn't fall down. Once this happened it was so overwhelming that I had to stop what I was doing and go lay down on my bedroom floor. Between the feeling like the world was spinning, my heart racing, my legs feeling like they would give out at any minute, I was sure I would pass out. It felt like a tidal wave rushing around inside my body. It also felt like the world was moving at high speed and I was moving in slow motion. I really thought I was losing it. I remember thinking, "This is not normal but I had no words for what was happening to me."

The rapid weight loss was another story. My colleagues and friends in my department at the university would daily tell me how "thin" I was. Of course I didn't see it because I was running around like that proverbial chicken… I was doing all the things and more so I didn't even notice how thin I was until I saw a picture of myself from that Christmas. I was shocked.

At some point I ended up going to the doctor. My friend and GP at the time Carleen (yes the same one from the Panera story) came into the room after I'd done the blood work and I will never forget what she said after she hugged me. "What is going on with you?" I had no idea what she was talking about. I thought I was just there to talk about new mom stress. Well, nope. Not quite that simple.

I described the hair falling out in the shower. It would come out in clumps in my hand, so much so I had bald spots next to my temples. She assured me that nothing that was happening to me was normal. Ugh!

She explained that due to the labs, it appeared that I had developed an autoimmune disease. Oh joy! I really had no idea what that was then, but I knew it wasn't good. She decided I needed more blood work and we'd then go from there. We did and she was correct.

Graves Disease

I was then diagnosed with Graves Disease. An autoimmune disease that sped up my system and made things go faster. Joy! Carleen referred me to an endocrinologist. That was the beginning of the tests and many many doctors visits. I started a medication regime. I took medication under monitoring so the levels could be adjusted (many times). Things were starting to smooth out and I felt less awful.

I also started reading everything I could on the subject because apparently this is a very common thing for women, although I'd never heard of it.

Fast forward to one year later. I'd been taking medication for Graves Disease and life was leveling out, well sort of. I was sitting in the back of my mothers car with Maya coming back from a trip to Minnesota. In a nanosecond, I knew something was off. I couldn't tell what it was, but I felt off. I was immediately light headed, my body started tingling, I had a fever, and was achy. All in a matter of minutes. I said to my mom, "What the hell is this now?" I described the symptoms. She told me to call my doctor when we got home. We were 30 miles away.

When we got home I immediately went to bed because I felt like I had the flu but worse. I called Carleen. I don't remember if she was available, but whoever I talked to told me that based on what I said I was having an allergic reaction to the thyroid medication I was on and to stop taking it immediately and come in for testing.

So I did.

The results of me "going in" were that I was in fact having an allergic reaction to the thyroid medication and my white blood cell count was dangerously low. The doctor I was dealing with likened it to, "someone with AIDS whose white blood cells go down" which means I wasn't able to fight off infections.

It was a "toxic" reaction.

Short story, I had to make a decision immediately about what to do. I was told I could have my thyroid removed (a thyroidectomy) or I could have it ablated (swallowing radioactive iodine to blast the shit out of it and basically kill my thyroid so it doesn't work anymore). I was also told that I had to choose one because thyroid cancer was also an option in my future. Again, yay!

I talked to Carleen while we were stretching one day after a spin class and I was still in decision making mode. She lovingly urged me to do the ablation due to the risks of the thyroidectomy, basically cutting near my vocal cords and other apparently pretty important (ha) veins, nerves, etc. She shared more and I was convinced. Now I needed to tell my family and schedule the procedure and plan for the after care. I made the appointment.

The next part was fun. I was told that I had to isolate myself after the procedure due to the radiation exposure and that I could not be around my daughter due to the radiation risks for her. What? More stress...

After talking to family and friends... I made a plan to go to the cities to have lunch with a friend and longtime fitness colleague and then return home and spend the night in my mother's basement so I would not be near anyone or cause them harm. I was told I had to cover the seat on the toilet, I had to use disposable gloves, dishes, and plastic ware and throw them away after I used them. What?

The radiation and potential for causing harm to anyone near me scared my mother so much she almost didn't let me stay in her basement. I didn't have an alternative so she let me stay there. I was cautious, I did what the doctors told me to do, but also felt very sad and alone.

So what really triggered this autoimmune in my overloaded system?

127

Here's my theory. This is my non-medical professional personal opinion, but I believe it in every cell of my body this is true. My life BC (before children) had been filled with ups and downs like every other person on this planet. However, for me, meaning being sexually assaulted in a variety of ways a variety of times, being raised by a single mom who to me, felt like she was there in body only and was always distracted by other things, moving to a city far away from friends at the age of 13, hormones and all the other things that stressed my little me system, all added up.

I should probably add in there that my birth father was not around. I'd never met him. Might be some underlying unconscious daddy or abandonment issues... hmmm.

Then coupled with all the stress in "older me"... college a variety of times, work, teaching fitness classes and working out, new marriage, wedding, second wedding, moving, sick pregnancy, scary birth, pets, finishing grad school, moving again... all the things that for some people don't phase them. Meaning their systems can handle it... it's not too much for them. It was too much for me.

My system said "NOPE" I'm done. And my thyroid decided to go from functional mode into dysfunctional mode. Dysfunction in my case led to disease...

Overall, not a big deal really, for me, however I can tell now when the levels are off because I gain weight, I get sluggish, I get more brain fog which isn't related to eating more or lack of movement or lack of sleep and I am very aware of it.

Overall this is really not a huge deal. Many many women have thyroid problems...

But knowing how my system responded to all that stress after all those years is an interesting take away. No one has ever told me this outright. I just know it to be true.

The thyroid issue became the catalyst for me learning how to start to listen to my body. I had to start paying attention to the signals my body was giving me. It may have been trying to talk to me earlier. If it was, I clearly wasn't listening, so it decided to talk louder.

Body talks. I have to listen.

Now, some 20 plus years later, both of my daughters have an autoimmune. They both have POTS (postural orthostatic tachycardia syndrome). Which has caused them endless hours of grief and has affected everything from daily living, to school performance and more.

I also now wonder, after knowing what I do about generational trauma, if their autoimmune is a result of my unprocessed trauma and stress and my mothers and so on? If it's how their system "inherited" things.

When Exercise Isn't Enough...

The first time I was aware that something was really off with me was on our families annual trip to Greece. When my youngest was two or three. The three of us, myself, my husband and my daughter Maya were staying at my mother in laws just outside of Athens. It was summer so it was hot and I had a toddler and was easily stressed out.

At the time we were in a taxi just outside my mother-in-law's home. It was noisy, hot, dusty and I was tired. I was in the back seat of the taxi and we were going somewhere with his sister and her daughter. Because there were so many of us in one vehicle we were tightly packed and I remember feeling very anxious and uncomfortable due to the noise, heat, and more.

What happened next startled me due to my reaction. I don't think anyone else in the car knew what was going on with me, but inside I felt like I was going to explode. My husband's niece's feet were touching my leg and it was making me crazy. I felt like I was losing my mind. I couldn't figure out why this very little thing was making me crazy and all I could do was keep gently asking her to move her feet. I did and she kept moving them back and touching me. I almost lost it. I remember feeling like I was gonna jump out of my skin, scream at her, or leap out of the taxi. Thank god I didn't. I have no idea what stopped me, but I didn't. I remember thinking, "What the hell is wrong with me, she's not doing anything wrong. I've got to be losing my mind."

Now, let me explain. His niece was very young and not doing anything abnormal. She was just being a child in a stuffed taxi on a hot day. I, on the other hand, was in emotional and sensory overload and that's all it took to send me over the edge. Being a new mom, in a country where it's so hot it would melt steel at times, I don't speak the language, being in a taxi with more people than should be allowed and no air conditioning, I was on tilt. My overly charged nervous system was on high alert and it was letting me know it didn't feel safe.

At the time I didn't understand anything about how we work, how trauma works and how the nervous system works. I just thought I was losing my mind. It scared me and because I didn't understand what was going on with me, I didn't share the experience with anyone. Who was I going to tell? When I was able to calm down, I was embarrassed at how I felt, and I just kept going. My reaction to the situation was out of proportion to what was happening.

The takeaway here is that my exercise rituals were not available to me when I was in Greece (at least at that time and for a variety of reasons) and my system noticeably felt the difference. I didn't have it to use a crutch (healthy crutch, but still a crutch) to manage my stress. When my movement practice wasn't available, I managed stress at a much lower degree. I'd become reliant on it. The benefits that exercise gave for me managing my "typical" daily stressors at home did not carry over for the times when I couldn't exercise. The magical effects were not long lasting.

Melina & Yoga

When Maya was two we brilliantly decided it was time to try for another baby. I say brilliantly because my body had other plans.

We started trying. I got pregnant not too long after.

Warning... this might be too graphic for some. Know I'm talking about a miscarriage and then skip three pages ahead.

I miscarried nine weeks in. It was horrible. The pain. The bleeding. I ended up going into the hospital for help and answers. I was admitted. They did an ultrasound and found nothing.

They what? Yes! They found nothing. Well they found "pieces of tissue."

I was in shock. How could they find nothing... "tissue isn't a baby" is what my brain kept saying, as the attending kept saying, "This happens all the time. It's normal" Meanwhile, I'm laying in the hospital bed still bleeding, confused, and sad. Oh?

I was then told to go home and that my body had "probably absorbed the rest of the tissue" and it would "get better over time."

WOW! What a relief! Thanks western/modern medicine.

I was hurting. I was sad. I was in pain (think horrific but bigger period cramps/contractions that pull you forward into fetal position). I was still bleeding. I had just lost what I thought was my baby and all they could say was… "it will get better."

You have got to be kidding me.

Within the next year, I was pregnant again and it happened again.

This time, it started the same way. Spotting. Cramping. Fear. What was different this time was that it was New Year's Eve. I called the hospital. They called my doctor, I think. I was told to try to make myself comfortable and… wait for it… "Keep the tissue when it passes and bring it to the clinic." Yup!

Being in pain and bleeding, sad, afraid, and coupled with all the other feelings of overwhelm swirling around in my being and on top of that I had to figure out how to "keep the tissue?!" WHAT?!

I was in shock.

It took hours. I sat in the shower and let the water pour down on my stomach to ease the pain as I had before with the contractions when I had Maya.

I was in and out of the shower a dozen times.

Sometime after midnight it happened.

I sat on the toilet. I passed the tissue. I fished it out of the toilet. I put it in a mason jar and put it in a paper bag and then put it in my car.

What happened after that I don't remember other than I'm fairly certain I went to bed and cried myself to sleep. At some point I took the tissue to the hospital lab.

Gross part over. I do know, in this 57-year-old brain and body, that miscarriages are common. My 30-year-old-something brain and body did not know that and that what happened to me was fairly common. But that doesn't mean it wasn't traumatic.

It was awful. Both times.

But I just kept going.

I went back to work. Went back to teaching. Went back to momming. Went back to taking care of the house. Nothing changed.

What I needed was to grieve. To allow the process of grieving to happen. I needed to take the time to really process and grieve the losses. But I didn't. I didn't know how and no one suggested that I do so.

We can do better. We have to do better. We have to support women better. Period.

15 years later I was in a TRE® continuing education workshop with Dr. Berceli, TRE®'s founder, and we were doing demonstrations. I'd volunteered and my body began to process some of the birth trauma I'd gone through. Dr. Berceli shared that in one of the countries he'd worked in that "when this happens to women" in that country, all the women gather and support each other. They cry, dance, hug, sob, scream, shake, and more, until the pain and suffering is released from her system and it stops. WOW! Now that's connection and support and love.

I was jealous and excited that somewhere in the world, women hold space for each other because they get it. It also speaks to community and connectedness, which is beautiful.

We can do better!

I was determined though to have this second baby. For many reasons.

For the next three years I worked with my doctor and we kept trying. I was referred to the infertility clinic. I hated that simply from the name, because I was not infertile. I had a child who I carried to term and is alive. I was not infertile.

One day when I was in the clinic waiting for a consult, I read an article on women, miscarriages, stress, and the benefits of yoga and acupuncture.

I went home and read everything I could find on the success rates of women who'd miscarried who then actively practiced yoga and stress management and who'd used acupuncture as a means of being able to carry a baby to term.

I also went down a yoga rabbit hole. I talked to my friends and colleagues from the gym about yoga. I started taking yoga classes from them. This was the beginning of my yoga life. At that time there were only a few articles online about the success rate and the "how to" to use acupuncture. I saved the article and knew I needed to ask the acupuncturist I'd worked with before if he'd be willing to try this method with me.

I asked and he said he would be willing to try the protocol. We agreed to stay in touch.

I also worked closely with my doctor and we agreed to try a procedure to "ensure" that the pregnancy would hold. We did a procedure that required my husband to "finish" his business in a cup and then they inserted it into me with a turkey baster and catheter like device.

Of course when the time came and I did get pregnant it wouldn't be quite that easy.

I became a regular yoga class attendee. I'd leave after teaching my Spin class and walk down to the next room where a colleague was teaching yoga. The tension in my body started to decrease. I became more flexible both physically and mentally. I also started having regular massages from friends who were going through Thai yoga massage training. That was delicious. I have the best friends.

We then made a plan to go into the doctor's office when I was ovulating. We'd have my husband do his thing and then they would very carefully place it inside me using a tube and whatever else they needed to inject it in me.

The very careful part was emphasized by the medical team. I did all the things I was supposed to do on my end to ensure it would be successful. I was calm. The room was dark and when the amazing being who was doing the procedure entered the room, she dropped the sample and the catheter on the floor. I panicked a little and she reassured me that it was ok. Oh universe…what a time to have a sense of humor.

I would then within 24 hours go to the acupuncturist, have that procedure done, and then hope and pray that it would work.

We did. It worked. I got pregnant.

Thank God! After all that…

Remember me having to "take in the tissue" from the second misscarriage? The test results came back that I had a possible blood clotting issue and if and when I got pregnant again I would have to take multiple medications and inject some medication into my stomach daily for a period of time. Yay!

I am not a fan of needles, but I didn't care. I'd do pretty much anything at that point to avoid having that pain of loss again. I knew I was meant to have a second child. I knew it in my bones.

After a while my growing belly started to look like I had a henna tattoo (like a chain necklace) drawn on my stomach with all the little bruises from the shots I had to give myself daily.

It was actually kind of funny.

She survived and she (Melina) was born, five and a half years after her sister. My second C-section was performed, as was planned. This time I knew what was going to happen and how rough the post surgery recovery would be. However I didn't plan how hard it would be to have a newborn and recover from a major surgery while parenting a five and a half year old.

I absolutely believe in every single cell of my being that it was the acupuncture procedure after the "injection of his sperm" and the beginning of my leap into the yoga world that kept her alive. A combination of Western medicine, Eastern medicine, and yoga to de-stress me.

I'm not discounting modern medicine and am grateful for what they did to help me, but I really believe it was the other two, let's say stress management tools and Eastern medicine that was the key to her survival.

Hmmm, stress being a cause of misscarriage?

When I tell people about my girls, I say I birthed art. They are both wicked talented, beautiful, and amazing creative beings and I'm lucky and honored to be their mom.

One of the biggest takeaways for me during that time of hell, well… moments of hell… was that I ultimately immersed myself in Yoga. It was the perfect marriage with my Spinning classes. The two paired magically. The much needed yin to the yang of the often intense Spinning classes and the stress it put on my body. I needed the endorphins, the movement, and the social connection with my colleagues and students. I loved the intensity, but that doesn't mean my body loved it all the time.

I took Yoga classes as often as I could when at the gym and time allowed. Ultimately when Maya was eight-ish and Melina was two I decided I needed to take the next step and dive deeper into Yoga and become a teacher. I knew I would not be going back to higher education, would financially benefit from teaching more classes, and was fascinated by the whole yoga world.

When I was trying to explain what Yoga was to my mother and why I was so drawn to it, I explained it as...

"A system of living that believed
the body was equally as important
as the mind and the spirit."

I was hooked and appreciated any practice that addressed the whole person as a system of living.

I was raised in the Presbyterian church – I was not a fan of sitting still and being quiet (that's another story, ha)... and nowhere ever did I remember the church and organized religion talk about the importance of taking care of the physical body.

I took the leap and started a year-long, weekend-based Yoga Teacher Training program in Minneapolis, Minnesota. My mom, along with a friend who was also a yoga teacher and soon-to-be Ayurveda Practitioner, agreed to help with the girls on the weekends so I could attend classes and workshops.

The practice of Yoga to me, over time, became much more than the asanas (postures or poses). That's how I was introduced to it, through friends and colleagues at the gym. It was movement based, and it felt good; and although my very tight and tense body struggled to do most of the postures in the beginning, I fell in love. It was powerful, profound, and brought the much needed peace to my body.

My first experience with yoga, even though at the time I had no idea that it was yoga, was at a fitness education conference in Chicago. I'd spent the weekend with my girls (fitness family) learning about the latest toys and training techniques to continue our education and expand our toolboxes as instructors.

After days of sweating, learning, and laughing, we ended up in one of the breakout rooms and sat on the floor in front of the presenter (Michelle LeMay) waiting for her to start the session. The energy in the room was different from all the other sessions we'd attended. It was quiet. There was no music blaring. The lights were dimmer and there was no equipment covering the room for us to use. This is one of those "the memory is etched in stone" moments in my brain. She was sitting on the stage in gomukhasana (cow face pose) which is a serious hip opener and at times impossible for those new to yoga.

As we sat on the floor right in front of the stage, I remember looking up at her, sitting with her legs crossed in this weird position. Without words she was encouraging and inviting us to sit the same way. I then, without missing a beat, actually laughed and said out loud, very loud, "You have got to be kidding me." My girls laughed and lovingly shushed me. I was dumbfounded at how she could sit like that because I knew my body would break in half before I would ever be able to sit like that.

I love foreshadowing!

As part of the yoga teacher training program, we studied yoga philosophy, yoga foundations, Sanskrit, the breakdown and reasoning behind the yoga postures, anatomy, and much more.

What I learned and ultimately began to understand and incorporate into my life was the philosophy of Yoga – not simply the postures, but its principles – as best as I could as a single mother living in the Midwest in the United States. It is a 5,000 year old system for living; a deep, rich, and profound system of living. It had guidelines to follow (similar to the 10 commandments from the Bible). It had mythology (similar to Greek Mythology). It was a system for living that incorporated the body and a sister science,

Ayurveda (ancient Indian holistic medical system that is based on the elements, food as medicine, and more.) It addresses energy. It addresses life and the human experience and how to best live it as a whole.

It was also a discipline. The discipline of practicing Yoga for me created the calm I craved. The chaos in my head craved calm. Discipline helped create calm. Chaos is the opposite of calm. Chaos when not balanced with calm creates challenges internally and externally.

As part of the training we also had to develop a personal practice and work closely with a mentor. My personal practice began to take shape every morning at the same time with me setting up space for myself (one Yoga mat and one block, which is all I could afford at the time.) I'd warm up and then have no idea what I was doing or what I was supposed to do next. I didn't trust myself to know what to do even months into the program, without being led by an instructor. I was also frustrated often because I knew that breathing (on purpose) was part of the practice and there were many times that I couldn't take a deep breath if my life depended on it. Hello, anxiety!

Over time all the pressure I was putting on myself to "know what to do" and "know how exactly to do it" and "to do it right" started to fade away and I began to learn how to trust myself. It also didn't hurt that my mentor, an amazing being and now one of my closest friends, Monique, helped me co-create a practice that not only worked for me, but was what my body needed to do. General education is great. Private lessons or something similar is magic because it's tailor made for you.

I was often shocked at how little I knew about the body after being a fitness instructor for some 30 years. The insights and new knowledge I gained were the proverbial icing on the cake for me when it came to my teaching skills and confidence. The other parts of the overall training I took to heart and began to embody deeply were the philosophies of living a meaningful and purposeful life. The Yamas and the Niyamas (10 guiding principles) made sense to me. A few specifically spoke to me: "do no harm" (ahimsa), "self study and reflection" (svadhyaya), and "the physical aspect" (asana). I began treating myself as I do others by practicing ahimsa towards myself... novel idea. I began to be able to sit or be still and quiet with myself... again, novel idea. The physical aspect or asana practice helped me grow emotionally as my body began to soften from the years of held tension and trauma and the stress of exercising seven days a week and often multiple times during the day if I was teaching.

It was the combination of my exercising (my teaching and my personal practice) and yoga that kept me sane though the next few years through divorce, single momming, and all the things that come with that lovely beautiful gnarly complicated mess called being a single mom who has her own shit.

TEACHABLE MOMENT

Having a Daily Personal Practice of movement that also doubles as stress management is non negotiable for me and I believe would benefit all women. Self care is not an indulgence, it's a discipline.

We cannot afford to not take care of ourselves, our bodies. Stress and trauma is a part of the human experience and will always be there. Actively managing it is the key. Your system can only handle so much before it starts to function at a lower level or not function at all. Eventually dysfunction turns to disease.

In life, there are **nice-to-haves** and **need-to-haves**. Our bodies are designed to move. That is a need. Without the balance of slowing down and stillness we perpetuate the fight or flight momentum. We need to foster rest and digest to balance us and also to connect with ourselves.

Balance is the key. Balancing requires that we slow down. Yoga (most forms, not all) encourages calming down the nervous system. Give your body the gift of slowing down with deep delicious stretching and strengthening both physically and emotionally. See what's out there that speaks to you. There is something for everyone from fitness yoga to restorative. Some move fast. Some move slow. Some are dedicated to rest and relaxation and some to laughter.

Lastly, find a qualified, trained teacher who resonates with you. If local, ask around, women will know...

people talk. If online, read the reviews. I view the different kinds of yoga out there like reading a book. You have to get to chapter two or three before making a judgment call and giving up. Try a few different flavors of yoga and a few different teachers before settling in.

Believe me it's worth it.

How to Become a Stress Mess & Medusa Meltdowns

L ife goes on right? As it does...

I navigated the divorce and single momming with the help of friends, family, exercise, yoga, and probably a lot of wine.... well a lot of wine... full disclosure.

I thought I was doing pretty well, but there were moments that, when I look back, make me think what an asshole I was or how could I do that or what was I thinking?

That's the catch phrase... the last line... "What was I thinking?"

The reality is that a lot of the time... when I was stressed... I was not thinking. I was reacting. Reacting versus responding. That's what stress and trauma can do to you. The emotional part of the brain takes over and the rational newer part goes off line.

My wicked stressed adult brain and my childhood traumatized brain made me react to situations as opposed to responding like a rational, loving, educated, calm adult who wants the best for her girls.

When Maya was in elementary school, her health started to go south. Anxiety and depression set in and along with it chronic stomach pain. I didn't understand this at the time so we spent countless hours and days at countless doctor's offices trying to figure out what was happening to her. Of course we did all the alternative health things as well. Nothing helped the pain.

Her health kept getting worse. Then more diagnosis came. Then more stress. Skin issues. Then more pain. More doctor visits. More tests. It was awful and I had no idea what was going on or what to do. I felt completely helpless and my stress about feeling helpless undoubtedly caused our house to be more stressed.

I don't remember reading about this in the very very very fine print at the bottom of the mom contract... that must have read: "You may have a child with health concerns that will take over your world... Congratulations and have fun with that."

I did everything to make sense of what was happening to her. Nothing helped. This poor baby of mine was prodded, poked, scoped, scanned, and pricked, never resulting in any answers or relief for her. She was diagnosed with so many things. She had two surgeries to find out what was causing her stomach pain. She had a GI scope at Mayo in Rochester and had a laparoscopy to see if it was endometriosis. No one had an answer and everyone gave either "We don't know" or a completely different diagnosis. And for those of you wondering if she tried meds? She did. We had her do the genotype testing to see "what med" was right for her. Disaster. She tried so many different meds that it was ridiculous and none of them did anything. Better yet, some made her symptoms worse.

The hindsight saying... "If I'd only known then..." My response to that is... trust your gut if you have a child with "undiagnosable health concerns." Listen to the child. Be patient. It's ok to take what the doctor says with that proverbial grain of salt if it seems off to you and love the child you have, including all the things. Unconditional love is magic. Fear stops everything.

Talk therapy – Yes we tried that too. But let's talk about this for a moment. For her this was a complete bust and made everything worse. She had two when she was young. The second (Tina) was magical and they connected and it did help her. However, the first therapist that she saw made everything 10 times worse. Which of course I did not know, meaning I had no idea they were not a good fit.

If you or anyone you know is seeing a therapist and it is NOT a good fit, get the hell out. Now. Find someone else. It's your right to do this. I had no idea back then that you could "shop around" for a better fit. I just assumed you worked with the therapist that you were assigned to. No, it's not that simple. I wish I'd known that back then. I never thought about it. No one told me...

We also did every alternative practice I could think of, including acupuncture, grain free/dairy free diet, supplements, essential oils, energy work, and on and on, and nothing made anything better. Some she responded to and was willing to repeat, some not. Her not feeling well affected everything in our house.

I also decided that it was time to maybe date again. I'll keep this short. I did. We got married two years later. It was a disaster. I learned up close and personal how and what mental health "concerns" can look like. We divorced within two years. That's all (for now).

The reason I mention the above little jaunt into more adulting, is that Maya was sick and she and her sister still needed me. I was still teaching 3-5 classes per week (Spin and Yoga), doing some other side gigs to earn money and taking care of the house.

What I didn't realize was that I was living in a perpetual really really high state of stress that ultimately led to overwhelm which... yup... you guessed it... directed my behaviors on occasion that I still cringe when I think about it. What happens to me when I get overwhelmed is a few things:

1. Anxiety kicks in
   Brain and body go into busy mode, multitasking
   – not manic – almost like what I imagine ADD to
   feel like. My breathing gets shallow. My heart rate
   increases. I feel panicky. I get overwhelmed from a
   sensory standpoint. When my anxiety is really high,
   small things like kitchen clutter is chaos. My favorite
   mental visual for when it used to get really bad – I'd
   feel like a pinball in a pinball machine being bounced
   around everywhere by a force that I couldn't control,
   until it stopped or I had a meltdown.

2. Pity party mode
   This is embarrassing and I know this is little me and
   teen me and the unresolved pain trying to get me to
   listen to her and/or having an emotional tantrum... I
   started listening recently to little me, talking to her,
   and asking her questions and boy does she have shit
   to say; she wants to be validated because I was not
   able to tell the story in "her" real time and because I
   was told by the legal system basically it either didn't
   happen or I couldn't take action because I was a
   minor. Teen me has a different tone altogether... she
   is snarky and angry and needs and wants attention.

3. React versus respond
   Meaning I act and speak before thinking... yup that
   always goes well.

4. Rage
   Slam doors, scream, blame, yup, this one's fun.

5. Migraine
   These show up when I push myself too much and
   there is an emotion from something in the past that
   needs to be released.

And it all happens simultaneously IF I don't take notice of it and then immediately get grounded and cry or if my self care/daily practice of stress management (movement) and general wellness is lagging.

I've spent years working on developing a personal practice for myself that is realistic, simple, and easy to do. I finally came to the realization that it's a simple equation STRESS GOES UP = SELF CARE GOES UP. It has to. My survival and quality of life depends on it.

In the last eight years I've learned enough to now understand how stress works, how trauma works, and the science behind them. I also now know my early warning signs of anxiety, overwhelm, and more and am continuing to work to be more mindful. To rest more. To do less. To just be, more often. To listen to and have conversations with my body.

Yes, I talk to my body. This is the area I'm currently working on. Asking my body what it needs. If it hurts, asking what it needs. What it wants. Plus, my daily personal practice of self care, self love, movement, vagus nerve toning practices, and conversations with the universe, these all help me regulate my nervous system and navigate my shit with more grace and ease. It will always be a process.

Before, though, it was bad and not understanding the shame and embarrassment was a lot to navigate. The worst moments are the ones I lovingly call my Mommy Medusa Moments.

Medusa is one of my favorite mythological beings. I don't really know why, I just really like her. Maybe it's the hair/curls. Maybe it's her power. Maybe it's her beauty. Maybe it's her mystery. She's dark, similar to the character Bellatrix in *Harry Potter*.

They both represent power and strength. If I spend too much time dissecting that, it'll be another book so… for now… There are a few Mommy Medusa Moments that I'm still working on forgiving myself for.

I bring up the two above because when I've had these meltdowns I think of these two women/characters and think… hmmm this is very likely how they would act. They both represent "the dark side." Since I like them both… It helps me give myself grace and lightens the yuck (shame).

The Mommy Medusa Moment that stands out the most to me is one day when I raged at Maya because she was not doing as I asked.

I was stressed and in a conversation with my second ex-husband (conversations with him were challenging at best) while Maya needed my attention. She was crawling on the floor and was not an infant. It happened so fast I couldn't believe it came out of my mouth.

I yelled something to the effect of, "unless your eyes are bleeding you better get up and walk." I froze, and, in an instant, couldn't believe I'd just uttered those words. I was mortified to have said that to my daughter. Yes, I did apologize profusely, but still the shame and embarrassment of saying that was crippling for a while. I felt like such an asshole for the next few days... well maybe still a little now... as I said it's a process of learning to forgive myself.

This is reacting versus responding. I was overloaded and blew up. Again just like I had at my mom when I told her about the abuse.

I've slammed many doors. I've thrown things. I've yelled. I'm human. But when those outbursts have an adverse effect on someone or something... that's not ok.

I did put a hole in a door one time by slamming it so hard it hit a mirror on the opposite wall. Try explaining that one to your children and the person you may have asked to help you fix the damage because you don't have those skills.

Embarrassment.

Being overwhelmed, sitting on the kitchen floor sobbing, slamming doors out of rage when shit just keeps happening and it's too much to handle... you get my point. Stored stress, trauma, and anxiety built up in my system like a pressure cooker until I ultimately exploded with words. There's only so much we as humans are designed to carry in our systems before we blow up, or worse...

I've blown up many times at my girls and I always hated myself after because I always felt like such a horrible person. I default to "who would do that to the people they love... I suck." And other negative feedback.

No one ever was physically hurt by my verbal explosions, but they were still in close proximity and their systems still picked it up. So even if I'm not directing the rage or verbal spewing at them, it still directly affects them. Not indirectly. Directly.

Writing this now, I can say I don't spew or have Mommy Medusa Moments any more or at least it's been years. But I am a work in progress, I am human, and life still continues to happen. My job as a human in progress is to continue to do my work. To actively manage my stress and traumas. To be a better mom.

I will still get stressed. I will still get overwhelmed. I will still sit on the kitchen floor or bedroom floor or any floor and cry when I need to or when life comes at me really hard and I will continue to work on my shit so it doesn't have an adverse effect on my children.

Life happens as it does and we do and say things that we don't always mean and/or deeply regret later. We do overreact. We do yell. We do slam doors and throw things and more. We do on occasion hurt those we love and typically it's not intentional. It's a reaction NOT a response. It happens very fast, like the volcano that was me that erupted when I told my mom about the assaults.

Part of the reason this happened was a result of me having little **interoception** (sense of internal sensations in your body, not only biologically, but emotionally as well) at the time. I was so distracted with the conversation I was in and having lived years of being in a **high functioning freeze** (a stress response that happens when we can't fight or flight but we still have to function… basically we're physically present but not really connected in the moment). I had no idea I was going to erupt this way. I've spent a lot of my life here. Being in a freeze served me at times. Not at others.

What can we do about this when it happens? Work on skills and use tools that help foster interoception so you can **self regulate**. Self regulation means knowing when too much is too much. Another concept we are not taught.

We can also do repair work and continue to work on ourselves through stress management, self reflection, self regulation, self exploration, and forgiveness.

My mom was in my kitchen one day years ago and said to me, as her mom said to her… "One day you'll be able to forgive yourself." Working on it!

REPAIR WORK is always a beautiful thing. Humility is a beautiful thing. Being human is hard at times. Own your shit. When you hurt someone. Stress out someone. Cause suffering to someone. Yell at someone. Say something horrible to someone. Do something to someone you love BUT you didn't MEAN TO DO HARM… OWN IT!

Take a breath. Take a walk. Cry. Let the tension out. Go for a run. Punch a pillow. Do something and then apologize like you mean it. BUT… wait for things to calm down first.

It takes roughly 20 minutes for the stress cycle to complete when it's activated in our systems. If the person you upset or hurt by accident is stressed, they probably won't be able to hear or process what you're saying. Wait. Give it time and then ask if you can say something or if they can give you a minute. Then look them in the eye if you can, and apologize. Maybe offer a hug. Give hugs only if they will allow you to and honor it if they won't... they need time. Don't ever force an apology or hug on someone. Apologize without an excuse as to why it happened. Excuses negate the apology.

You're human. Shit happens. When shit happens, own it. And if you have a history of inadvertently hurting those around you but "not on purpose"... there is no time like the present. Start now.

If the shame is too great, because that's what happens to a lot of us when we behave like this, and you can't apologize with your words, or the person/people you caused harm to, won't talk to you... find other ways to apologize and own it.

Write it down. Leave a post-it in a place you know they will see it. Hell, leave 10.

Find out what their Love Language is and show them how sorry you are in a way that speaks to them. And then... learn from it. Use it as your own teachable moment. Ask yourself why did this happen? What's going on that pushed me to that edge? Accept that it was something inside you that triggered the meltdown or the volcanic eruption... not something someone else did.

TEACHABLE MOMENT

Life does not stop happening. We **can** control the chaos on the inside (it can be fun) with awareness and action using the right tools. Our nervous systems were designed forever ago. It's ridiculous to think that it should be expected to operate and function the same way given the speed that our world changes and the litany of unhealthy things our world offers us. We are meant to go in and out of these states (fight or flight, rest and digest) not hover in fight or flight more often than not.

Overreacting happens when our system is overloaded. When it's too much and needs to process and release some of the emotional tension/energy. Regardless of your intentions, those around you pick up on your (stress, anxiety) energy through **neuroception**.

Once I understood neuroception (and generational trauma, how my ancestors processed their stress), imagine the holy shit moment I had when I realized my daughter's health issues could have been inadvertently caused by me.

If you have a daily personal practice that helps nurture your nervous system, calms down the nervous system rather than elevating it, if you proactively bank your calm, you will be able to more easily access it later. Your resilience will increase and you will begin to respond more than you react. Life gets easier.

Having easy quick tools that help keep you grounded and help regulate your nervous system can be a game changer when it comes to over-the-top emotions, trauma responses, and nervous system overload. Some of my favorites are:

- 4-7-8 breath (inhale for 4, hold for 7, exhale for 8)
- Sighing breath (inhale and sigh out loud on your exhale)
- Lion's breath (inhale and exhale out loud, stick out your tongue and say "ahhhh")
- Run, do jumping jacks, do burpees, get your heart rate up
- Cry
- Get grounded with Child's Pose
- Wrap yourself up in a weighted blanket
- Practice TRE®
- Practice Vagal Toning Exercises (laugh, hum, gargle)

Do your work to regulate your nervous system. Do Repair work.

Practice Self Regulation and **cultivate** and foster your body awareness... **so you know when too much is too much. Have a general understanding of how and why these things work and then do the work to create healthy habits that regulate your system, because we know your children are picking up on your shit.**

Making Sense
of Me

feeling
healing &
trauma education

It started with a phone call from my mother. She said she'd just done "this thing" with her friend in Arizona while she was on vacation, and I "NEEDED" to do it for myself and my clients. It had something to do with the body. She finished by saying, "There's a training coming up in Madison. "I'm paying for it and you're going!" Excuse me… what?

I had no idea what she was talking about. This "thing" was called TRE®, which stands for Tension, Stress, and Trauma Releasing Exercises. This was in 2014 and by then I'd been teaching Group Fitness, Spinning, and Yoga classes for almost 25 years. I assume since the title had "exercise" in it my mother thought it was a good fit for me. To clarify, TRE® is not an exercise program.

In 2014, I was heading into my second divorce, broke, single, parenting two amazing, beautiful talented daughters, trying to figure out how I got there, and stressed all the time. I was teaching community-based Yoga for Employee Wellness programs and teaching private lessons for a living and trying to find more sustainable employment. I looked online to see if I could get a visual about what she was talking about. I had never heard of TRE®. When I looked it up, I found one video of a woman teaching it to another woman and what looked like a fairly new website with a little information and not much more. I was curious. I did sign up. I did go to the training a few months later. I had no idea what I was in for or the impact the "thing" would have on my life.

It wasn't long before I was in Madison at the venue for the TRE® training, standing in line with many others, getting my folder, name tag, and signing a lot of papers. Next, I remember sitting with roughly 40 or more others in a conference room, watching the organizer and a few others chat and then being introduced to the founder of TRE®, Dr. David Berceli. Dr. Berceli gave his presentation. His slides explained how he developed TRE® and the science behind it. I remember thinking to myself, after a few slides, "What is he talking about?" and "I am so out of my league here." The slides for that section of the presentation were fairly science heavy and I didn't understand anything he was saying, as I had no reference at that time about neurology, how the brain works, how trauma affects the brain, and more. It reminded me of Stats class in grad school. Not my favorite.

I felt so dumb because it was hard for me to understand the science that he was discussing because my anxiety was high at the time. It also fed into my "I'm too dumb to understand this" inner critic.

Right on cue as I'd done often in my life, I'd had an exit plan and I heard my lovely critic say, "Ok, stay until the break, then you can leave and no one will notice." Shortly after, as luck would have it, the theme of the slides changed to anatomy. This I understood! Whew! Dr. Berceli had great pictures and my anxious, self-doubting, hyper, self-critical brain calmed the f--- down. So I stayed longer. Oh my god am I glad I stayed! My life changed in many ways after that weekend.

Then we practiced TRE®. It was weird. It was magic. It was profound. The short version of the story is I was laying on the floor with the other 40 plus people there and we were shaking or vibrating or whatever you wanna call it. Some people were laughing, some people crying, some were quietly talking (the ones who'd done it before), and more. I remember looking around to see what the other people were doing because I heard noises I couldn't determine. We were instructed that it was ok to look around, but that it was best to remember to breathe and try and focus on ourselves. I did and this "thing" felt like a massage from the inside out. I'd never felt anything like this in my life. It also felt normal and natural, but I couldn't explain why.

Dr. Berceli and the other trainers were walking around observing, checking in, and quietly talking to some of us on the floor. I remember being sad and I wasn't sure why. I also remember feeling like I couldn't take a deep breath. I was breathing but it felt shallow and stuck in my chest. That was weird for me as a yoga and exercise person. I didn't remember ever having that feeling before, except when I took a breathing class.

As my breathing became more challenged, Dr. Berceli walked by. He must have sensed something was a little off with me. I'm certain I had a weird look on my face, I don't have a poker face. He knelt down and asked how I was feeling. His voice was calming. I remember telling him that I felt like I couldn't take a deep breath and how weird it was for me. He asked if he could try to help. I said yes PLEASE. I loved hands-on modifications from teachers at other fitness and yoga conferences. I was game for anything, plus it always felt so good to have someone make physical adjustments to your body that helped it move and feel better. He then, as I now know, did an intervention. He applied gentle pressure to a restricted place near my diaphragm. How he knew what to and in that specific place blew my mind at that time. He told me to inhale. I did. Then he applied gentle pressure to an area on my sternum and I was told to exhale. I did. And then... I took the DEEPEST

BREATH I'd ever taken in my life. Or at least that's what it felt like at the time.

This blew my mind. I was shocked. I was relieved and then I started to cry. I let the crying happen which, for me, prior to that, crying in public was not ok. It was as if my entire body let go. He gently suggested I roll to my side and rest. I did. I cried more quietly and for whatever reason, I knew that my life had changed because something shifted in my body. I felt unstuck. I was in the right place. I wasn't sure why, but I knew I was. That began my training to be able to teach others this amazing body-based healing tool.

So what is TRE® really? The short version is that TRE® is a universal body-based healing and wellness tool that is a series of seven simple exercises that anybody can do anywhere. It activates our primitive reflexes that bring us out of fight or flight. It can help release stress and trauma, increase resilience, decrease reactivity, decrease anxiety, it helps regulate our nervous system, and much, much more. Doing the template (the seven exercises) as we call it is the fun, easy part and it feels good.

When I'm asked "What do you do in a TRE® session?," I hear myself saying, "We do a series of movements that stretch and stress certain parts of the body and then we lay on the floor and shake or tremor." Insert smile here... I wait to see the look on someone's face after they hear this. This is usually when most people give me a "wait, what?" look and then I explain further that the shaking or vibrating or shimmying or tremoring, whatever you want to call it, is natural for the body to do and is the completion of the stress cycle.

If you've ever seen a dog shake from fear, it's the same thing. Think about when dogs are scared from loud noises like the 4th of July or during a thunderstorm. My dogs' behavior changes drastically when they are scared. They tremor, hide, become overly clingy, they begin to pant or pace or both. The dogs don't know it's "weird" or "looks weird" because they're dogs, so they don't stop it from happening.

Most people relate to this one and say, "Oh, ok, makes sense I've seen that," or "My dog does that." I then go into my litany of how amazing it feels, what it's done for me on a physical and an emotional level. Their eyes get big and the response is always, I need to try that, and so does (someone they know and love), and then I hear all the stories of why "they" need it. That is TRE® in a nutshell. But there's more.

What this brilliant method of stress and trauma management is also, is a tool for so much more. It's helped me connect with myself on a deliciously deep level. It's given me the best "trauma informed" education I could ever ask for, has helped me heal and has helped make sense of my life. By that I mean my thoughts, feelings, and behaviors that, in more times than I want to admit, didn't make sense. They weren't rational. They were "reactional."

So why was this so transformational for me (and thousands of others worldwide)? Because of the sexual assault and my nervous system not feeling that I was safe. Because I've lived with unprocessed traumatic emotions stuck in my body for most of my life. Our bodies store emotions in all of our parts. Our muscles, our fascia, our bones, our organs, our cells. Everything.

I also have PTSD. I don't have a formal PTSD diagnosis, so why and how dare I say I have PTSD without the formal testing, formal diagnosis, and documentation? Because I know I do. Also because of the countless, amazing, and highly talented mental health professionals I know, work with, and have discussed this with at *length*; they all confirm it.

If you look at the markers (characteristics) on the various sites that are devoted to PTSD, I meet a lot of them, or have at one time or another. Symptoms vary over time. Mine do and have diminished greatly over time based on the amount of work I do on and for myself.

The other reason for the "no formal diagnosis" is that when I told my mother what happened, when I was 16, she filed a lawsuit on my behalf, I started therapy and more, we (we meaning the world) didn't know enough about PTSD then. Its only recently that sexual assault survivors are given a diagnoses of PTSD in the hope to offer the support they need. Prior to that it was for military personnel only. By then, I mean in the mid to late 80s. Once I became familiar with the markers of PTSD it helped make sense of many things. I'm not attached to the phrase, however naming it releases some of the hold it has.

> *"If children experience trauma while the brain is in its developmental stages, the temporary traumatic trait needed to survive the trauma will be built into the brain as a permanent trait. Therefore if the child grows up in a traumatic environment, the more it is forced to use traumatic thinking patterns, the more those patterns will be embedded into their natural thought processes. Traumatized children will now begin to process all unfamiliar and overwhelming events as though they have the potential to be dangerously traumatizing. Their reactions will be naturally over reactive to normal events, causing hyperarousal or dissociative symptoms or behaviors."*
> Dr. David Berceli, TRE® Founder,
> from *Trauma Releasing Exercises (TRE®): A Revolutionary new method for stress/trauma recovery* (2005)

Had we known then what we know now, in 2023, about trauma and the physiological and neurological effects it has on us, things may have been different for me. But, if they were different I may not have landed where I am today. I wouldn't have the stories I have. I wouldn't have had my amazing, beautiful, colorful, sometimes drama-filled life. I wouldn't be able to do the work that I do. It may have been easier at times. Who knows...

This amazing tool helped me navigate and heal deeply like nothing else ever has. It got to the underlying deep issue that talk therapy, exercise, yoga, and everything else I've done in my life to heal this wound couldn't do. It was and still is the tool that addressed that deep deep inner part of me that no one sees and that I couldn't access. It activated the proverbial "inner healer" in me.

This tool that helps us do the emotional deep dive without talking about or reliving the story is one of the best kept secrets in the healing world. Similar to the ACE study ("the largest public health study no one's ever heard of"). Similar to that. The inner healer in us is a vibration and it helps us get unstuck. The vibration is movement itself. Movement heals. Women who are childhood sexual assault survivors and the women who love and support them need this tool in their toolbox. Well everyone does...

This tool or method heals us from the inside out. The vibration or tremor mechanism that is activated through the seven exercises releases tension in the physical and emotional structure of the body. When the body doesn't feel safe, it contracts, it tenses. When the body does feel safe, it relaxes.

"If frightening sensations are not given the time and attention they need to move through the body and resolve or dissolve, the individual will continue to be gripped by fear."
- Peter Levine, Psychotherapist, Author

The vibration (tremor) that is activated by practicing TRE® is the internal healing mechanism that we all have hard wired within us. The vibration and or external shaking (that is visible) can foster a sense of calm on the inside. We are well and whole when our inner state matches our outer form. Calm on the inside allows for us to be present, to feel lighter in our bodies, and show up in the world.

What has TRE® done for me on a personal level?

From an educational standpoint (I am an educator at heart and love to learn) it's helped me understand my sometimes very irrational and embarrassing behavior. It helped me understand what we call the trauma personality or my dark side as I lovingly call it (my trauma drama and my depression).

What I now understand through years of studying trauma, is that what happened to my nervous system and body as a result of the assault affected my brain. It essentially rewired my brain to be on a high alert (fight or flight, freeze and fawn) state more often than not. It also put me into a default state, an emotional freeze. Because "feeling" way back then was not an option. I needed to be in a "freeze" state to be safe (think about the animals that "play dead" in order to survive a predator). Both my nervous system and parts of my body that were touched during the assaults went into a freeze. Yes, an emotional freeze in parts of my physical body.

How can body parts be in an emotional freeze state? Because our bodies carry our emotions. We have issues in our tissues. Think about the feeling of joy. Think about that pit in your stomach when something is off or weird. Think about the phrase "gut intuition." Think about when you walk into a room and you know something is off.

If I think about the parts of my physical body that have been hurt over the years or were touched and not by invitation, they are injured. They are hurt. My stomach, where the C section scar is, holds fear. My stomach, where the laparoscopy scar is from attempting to eradicate endometriosis, holds fear. It's tight where the scar tissue is. Fear causes tension. My knee that was wrapped around a stick shift in a car accident in college and had to be surgically put back together holds fear. These parts were segmented from the rest of me.

"Trauma is the disconnection
from our authentic self...
healing is the reconnection with it."
Gabor Maté

The parts of my body that were touched by Rick are frozen and don't function as well as the other parts that are nearby. Case in point. With all of those years of teaching fitness classes and exercising, I could never understand why my hamstrings, inner thighs. and bum muscles didn't fire or respond like the other muscles in my legs. Those are the muscles he touched. Meaning I could not feel them fully because they were frozen.

In order for these muscles to function (fire correctly) like their counterparts, I have to give them extra attention. I have to work at strengthening and lengthening them slowly and methodically. These parts that were touched by him went into an emotional freeze (fear). They are weaker and require attention to get them to wake up and do what they need to do to work in conjunction with the rest of my body. With some muscles asleep, for lack of a better term, that creates imbalances in my body.

For years, my body carried a lot of fear in it. The work is to help my body feel safe, protected, and strong so that the entirety of me works as a whole, not separate parts. Trauma fragments us. We have to do the work to bring us back to wholeness.

For some of us who've had shit happen to us as children, our system wasn't able to tolerate it and feel supported. When this happens the neurological "switch" from safe to unsafe goes off all the time.

This is when shit happens. We become hard wired to be on alert more than we should and it's not something that we can control.

No one, at least no one I know, wakes up in the morning and says, "I think I'll be an asshole today. I'll be easily overwhelmed, I'll over-react, I'll yell at people I love, and then I'll beat myself up and feel like crap for the next several hours or days or longer because I made someone I love feel bad." It's awful!

Or the other shit happens. By this, I mean triggers. Triggers happen. I wasn't cognitively aware of what a trigger was until recently (three to four years ago when I began working in the mental health world as a Provider). On a physical level I was.

A trigger according to the National Alliance on Mental Illness (NAMI) is "sometimes referred to as a stressor, is an action or situation that can lead to an adverse emotional reaction. In the context of mental illness, referring to triggers usually means something that has brought on or worsened symptoms."

We all have triggers, things that set us off and I believe and they teach us lessons. They are our teachers. I have a few of these lovely things. They show up when I'm tired, when I'm stressed and haven't taken enough time for myself or put appropriate boundaries in place. When you couple living in a society that values the "go go go, do do do, be be be" with any unprocessed childhood emotions… that's a potential recipe for even more self inflicted stress. They are directly and indirectly related.

When I'm not well, my resilience (capacity to handle things) goes down, so things get to me a lot easier. My stressors are money, men, time, and my children being not well. Part of these triggers are mine, part I inherited from my mother, my father, my grandparents, and their parents and so on. From an epigenetic perspective that could be countless generations back. How my ancestors processed (or didn't) their stress is in my genes as well.

Money is a huge one, and being self-employed there's just a LITTLE stress... right (eye roll here). There's a LOT of money stress... depending on the day, week, month. Some days I manage it really well. I trust the universe has my back and I roll with it. Other days it lays me out and puts me in panic mode. It all depends on how calm I am inside. How regulated I am.

So, triggers... How do they show up? What does it look and feel like? A variety of things can happen, not all at once, and never in any sort of logical order, so I really have to pay attention because when I don't my body yells at me until I do pay attention and act on it. Let me explain.

When it does happen, my early warning signs start with anxiety. I get overwhelmed with "all the things" (whatever those things are at the moment). My heart starts to race and my thinking gets fuzzy. This usually means that I haven't paced myself, done enough self-care, gotten enough sleep, drank enough water, exercised, practiced TRE®, and/or all the other things I do to regulate my system.

If I'm at home, the first warning sign is that I get visually overloaded. Clutter starts to stress me out. Clutter is chaos to my overtaxed brain. If my internal state is in chaos, visual chaos makes it worse. This also makes me a fantastic organizer (the flip side of triggers and trauma).

Some days, just looking at all the (neatly unorganized... ha) paper piles in my kitchen, dirty dishes in the sink, dog hair on the floor, piles of shoes, coats on chairs, and too many other *things* cause more stress. When I'm stressed, my resilience for clutter is down and it makes me crazy. If I have the capacity, I can breathe and start to clear the clutter calmly. If not, it's like I suddenly develop ADHD and start pivoting from place to place picking up, throwing away, sweeping, rinsing... It feels like I'm the ball in a pinball machine being flung from one side of the machine to the other. It sucks and that's just the visual effects.

I also can't concentrate and my thinking is fuzzy; things like problem solving or paying attention to small details does not go well. This happened a lot in college, especially during exams or when giving a presentation or trying to understand accounting and stats. I'm also tired more and need more sleep. I start watching more TV at night because reading is too hard for my eyes to focus on.

I'm now, after eight years of practicing TRE® and teaching TRE® to others, training others to teach TRE® so the magic continues to spread and my resilience is up and I function at a greater emotional level than I ever have before. Eight years ago I was unaware of how the assault impacted my nervous system; it wasn't (and still isn't) common knowledge to the masses that this is how it works.

I understand now about what happened to me as a result of the assault was how it affected my brain – it essentially rewired my brain to be on "high alert" (fight or flight, freeze and fawn) more often than not. Here's the simplified version of how our stress and trauma system work.

1. an event happens
2. the autonomic nervous system (built-in safety system) views it as a threat
3. we go from rest and digest (connect)
4. to fight or flight, dissociate, freeze or fawn (protect)
5. a natural series of events then happen in the body to keep us safe
6. the rational (calm, clear, thinking, newer) part of the brain goes off-line
7. the other part of the brain (primitive, reactive, designed to save our lives from dinosaurs) takes over
8. adrenaline and cortisol are released to activate our built-in safety system
9. breathing changes, heart rate increases, senses heightened
10. blood flows to major muscles so they can prepare for flight or fight
11. some organs not necessary for life saving at the moment (below the diaphragm) decrease activity
12. we freeze or fawn (numb out and or people please) the other defense mechanism to save us from harm
13. once the threat is gone our system calms down and "goes back to normal" or to connect mode

We have this internal safety system built-in to keep us safe and we are designed to flow through those states on a daily basis. When that switch goes off or defaults to fight or flight, freeze, fawn (protect) more than it does to rest and digest (connect) when it's really not needed this is when things can go south. We used that at a time when it served us. However it becomes a problem when those survival behaviors kick in and it doesn't serve us. This is the Personality of Trauma.

The good news is IF we can understand how it works, it can give us grace, it can help us be more gentle with ourselves and others. It is an explanation of why and how we are the way we are. Not an excuse.

If you're curious and want to learn more about how the brain works during trauma, look up Dr. Dan Siegel and the "flipping your lid" theory or keep reading and I'll get to that later.

When was the first time I realized TRE® had a magical effect on me? I was asked to speak at a Women's Business Conference by a friend and the then Director, on "Self-Care Is A Discipline Not An Indulgence" for Women in Business. One of my favorite topics to talk about.

I was running late to the event, not for my presentation. I wanted to see the vendors, listen to a presentation or two, get set up, and be as ready as I could be. I left work, got stuck in traffic, and ended up circling the parking lot by the event center. Historically time is a

HUGE trigger for me. I have always had to be on time or, even better, early. I used to get razzed by a friend for always being early. Because if I'm early, then I can't be late right? If I wasn't early, I was late.

The parking lot was packed. I could not find a spot and the closest spots were blocks away. I had materials to carry in. Ahhhhh… Typically this would freak me out. My heart would start racing, I would panic, anxiety would take over and my breathing would get really shallow, almost as if I was holding my breath. I used to call it the "inner rev"… sort of like a car's engine starting to rev a little when in park and your foot is on the gas. The more pressure you put on the pedal, the more the car revs, but it doesn't go anywhere. Not something you see, but definitely something you feel.

As I was circling the parking lot I was waiting for this very familiar, automatic shitty feeling to kick in. It didn't. I was calm. What? I was calm. The inner rev didn't kick in. I checked again. I stopped the car, I took a breath, I had to check. It wasn't there. I was calm, I was present, I was thinking clearly and not panicking. I smiled and actually looked around as if to say to anyone looking at me… "do you see this?" My heart wasn't racing. What? I was blown away. How could this be? It had always been there when I felt like I was late, well at least as far back as I can remember. As I kept looking for a spot to park, the only thing that came to mind was how? How is this real? What's changed?

This was not my normal!

I sent a text to my friend Sue who was helping me with the presentation, telling her I was running a little late and then found a spot. I sat in the car for a few minutes thinking about how amazing it had felt to not have the panic rev kick in. I was calm, I was clear headed, I was not in freak out mode. I almost cried. At that moment it hit me. It was TRE®. That was the ONLY thing that I was doing differently. Nothing else in my life was new. My daily personal practice of self-care (exercise, yoga, laughing, good food, etc.) had not changed. I wasn't taking a new pill. My crazy busy life as a single mom had not changed. It had to be TRE®. I was beyond grateful.

We'd studied this in TRE® training. The idea that TRE® helps regulate the Central Nervous System by activating a natural vibration system we have built. This vibration or shaking helps complete the stress cycle (releasing the adrenaline and cortisol from the stress response) and gets us into our Parasympathetic Nervous System (rest, digest or "connect") versus our Sympathetic Nervous System (fight, flight or "protect"). I was internally calm and not overreacting. Seriously? It had changed or eliminated one of my triggers. I was in shock. Ecstatic and in shock. I couldn't wait to tell someone.

Ultimately what this healing and wellness tool does is to help activate our inner healer. It moves internal tension, stress, and trauma (physical and emotional) out of our body. The body needs to heal for us to be whole. It needs to release the hurt, the sad, the fear, and the anger so it can make room for happier, lighter energy.

Feeling Fear for the First Time (almost)
It's weird to say and even to think this, but with all the things that have happened to me over the years, I don't have any memories of actually feeling fear. My only clear memory of feeling fear and knowing I should be afraid from childhood was during the second assault since I knew what was going to happen. The other times in adulthood were Maya's birth and during harsh words in an argument with my girls' father.

That's why this is significant. Some time during my first divorce... I was walking with two family members one day and we were talking about my divorce. They were asking me questions about my daughters and other questions that family members would ask while a divorce is going on. As we walked and talked, I remember having this wave come over me like a tidal wave and I stopped, my hands started shaking and my breath got really shallow. My senses were on high alert. I froze and couldn't move. It was weird. They noticed something was off about me and asked what was going on. When I shared what was happening with me, I remember hearing myself say, "I'm afraid and I don't remember feeling fear before, how weird is that." They both agreed it was weird and we went on walking. This sense of fear felt very new to me and I wasn't sure what to do with it. There was also no danger to me at the moment. There were no tigers or bears in the vicinity about to chase me. I was for all other purposes physically safe.

As part of the drama from the divorce, the only other time I remember feeling fear was when my soon-to-be ex-husband made threats that he would take away my children and by that I mean to another country. He was stressed. I was stressed. I don't actually believe he would have, however, at the moment, I was terrified and had no recourse if he decided to do so.

Stress makes us all say and do things differently than when we are calm and rational. His stress coupled with my stress was a ridiculous mess.

Again, it is very "normal" (I hate this word) to feel fear in massively stressful situations like a bad divorce. The rub is me NOT remembering or feeling fear before this, in my mid-30s. I was functioning for far too long in an emotionally frozen state.

TEACHABLE MOMENT

If any of the things said here resonate with you, you are in amazing company. There are millions of women out there from all over the world dealing with stress and unprocessed trauma in their bodies. Millions of brilliant, beautiful women who on occasion (or more) act out of character, who get overwhelmed easily, who have bad relationships on a repeat loop, who react versus respond, who are too sensitive, who isolate, who numb out because that's the only thing that is available to them or what they've seen modeled. This is trauma drama. Take solace in knowing that these thoughts, feelings, and actions aren't a life sentence. They are the result of your system doing its job, but the job is on a tilt. It's spinning out. It's working way too hard when it doesn't need to. There are ways to help balance out our overly active system to calm the chaos. Practicing TRE® is one of the ways to help regulate it. To bring you and all of your parts back to wholeness. This massage from the inside out is easy to do and can be done anywhere at any time. You can find videos, research, providers, and trainers at www.traumaprevention.com.

*"More stress equals
more self care...
simple equation."*
- *Christine Varnavas*

History & Generational Healing

let's leave

a

legacy of love

I don't remember the situation, what led to my mom being in bed. She was either sick with a migraine, her undiagnosed Lupus was acting up, or an election had just gone to the "other team." Regardless, she was in bed and I'd gone over to talk, vent, spew about what was going on in my life at the moment, because spewing feels good and helps to get the words out. I'm sure I was spewing about husband number two.

As I was leaving her bedroom feeling better after venting, she said to me and I quote, "There've always been two things my whole life that have laid me out and make me feel like swiss cheese: money and men, and I think I may have passed that on to you." She then said, "I'm sorry honey. I don't know what else to say, other than you're so strong and you'll get through this."

I paused, took a deep breath in, and said, "Thanks, Mom." Shook my head and probably rolled my eyes. Then I left. In that moment there was no doubt in my mind that she was right. EVERY BONE IN MY BODY KNEW THIS WAS TRUE. I just didn't have the words to be able to understand or even explain it. I had inherited these amazing qualities from her.

For as long as I can remember, men and relationships have been hard. The money part hadn't really affected me too much by then because I'd always had enough to support myself either by working and living as a college student on financial aid or a car accident settlement money (I was a passenger in a car accident in college) or working full time plus my side gig of teaching fitness and yoga classes. My money insecurities didn't start until the divorce from my girls' father and I became a single mom employed only part time.

The men and relationships thing, however... I can always remember it being hard for me. I often heard myself say, "I don't do relationships well." Or, "Men hurt you then leave you." That was my mantra and my history. As was the case with my father – hurting my mother, never being there or either of us; my step father – sexual assault; boyfriends and partners – who may have behaved badly or just disappeared completely.

Somewhere close to 25 years ago I was in a short term (very short term) relationship with one man who I thought was pretty damn awesome. He was an Engineer and had the most amazing eyes and smile. We dated for a short while. We went out on real dates. Not just a bar hook up. We danced. He took me out for dinner. We laughed a lot. And then… one day… after maybe a month of dating, he simply disappeared.

No phone call at the agreed time. He didn't return my calls. No nothing. He just disappeared and I was heartbroken and confused. Why would someone do that? What happened? Did I do something? This of course fed right into my "you're not good enough" BS.

I later learned from him what had happened and bravo to him for having the bravery to reach out and tell me that it was him and not me. He'd reconciled with an old girlfriend and didn't want to hurt me so instead of telling me, he "just disappeared."

He initially took the easy way out; he ran. This was his emotional running from an uncomfortable situation. It was easier for him to run than to face it. But ultimately he did; he reached out and told me what happened and apologized. I still respect him for that. Repair work is a good thing.

I've had what I would call three major relationships. First love and two marriages. Ranging from two to ten years in length.

Relationships were always confusing to me. Why did some work and why did some not? I've wondered why my grandparents and great aunt and uncle have what appeared to be good relationships. Why do my aunt and uncle work so well together? Why did my mom's first two marriages end in divorce? Why was my dad married four times? Why was my brother's father (predator) married five times?

I thought I had it all figured out when I met my second husband. I had done so much work on myself. I'd gone through therapy. I'd done Eye Movement Desensitization Reprocessing (EMDR), a psychotherapy treatment that was originally designed to alleviate the distress associated with traumatic memories. The first time I did it was when it was relatively new on the therapy scene. It did nothing for me. However, the second time I tried it I definitely gained insights.

I'd gone through yoga teacher training. I'd read Pema Chodron's When Things Fall Apart and Crazy Making and other books recommended to me to heal. I'd done all the things. I had evolved. I'd grown. I'd done the work. So I thought...

When I met my second husband I had a list of relationships that I aspired to be like in my journal. He was impressed and agreed with me that everything I wanted in a relationship he wanted as well.

Needless to say, that marriage ended within two years for a variety of reasons.

In the beginning it was wonderful. Or so I thought. A lot of chemistry, but even more drama. Having looked back there were red flags that I chose to ignore because he was doing all the right things, buying me gifts and the emotionally addictive needy me ate it up like candy again. So much for "I'd grown." I was right back where I was before. Well, almost.

The intense attention he paid to me ended and reality set in. The red flags that I ignored, or better yet didn't fully understand, were front and center and making life ridiculously hard.

What had happened? Why would this happen again? More lessons needed to be learned.

It was happening again. The attraction, the attention, was intoxicating and then it ended.

If any man (well almost any man) even paid the slightest amount of attention to me, I was hooked. It was like a vacuum. They would show some kind of interest. I would melt like butter and then I was sucked in. I had no idea who I was or what I wanted. I also had no idea what I wanted in a partner, nor had I ever taken the time to think about what I wanted in a partner or a relationship.

I was like an emotional sponge. They magically showed up. They attended. They offered. They gave. And I ate it up like I'd never eaten anything quite like that before in my life and it filled me up. Emotionally, physically, and spiritually. I would become dependent on it. I started to crave it. It was like a drug. The attention was intoxicating.

Imagine something that makes you feel like you're flying or floating and life is beautiful. Life is good. Life is easy. You feel good about yourself. You are loved. It was like a drug. I craved it. It was like a high.

I needed it and when it wasn't there it was like going through withdrawal. My thoughts, feelings, and behaviors would change. It was like having a weird addiction to this person who I wasn't even sure I really wanted to be with. It was the attention more than the attraction that I was addicted to.

This is not me saying that I didn't love these men, I did in time and I believe things happen for a reason. However, the reason we got married in the first place may not have been ideal for a long term loving equal partnership. It was, however, the way I operated. By having someone interested in me, that meant I must be worth liking or loving. Ugh!

Both marriages were with men who went above and beyond what I would call the pursuit phase. They went out of their way to impress me with gifts and more and I allowed those gestures to blind me from the red flags I'd otherwise hope to see.

The underlying thread here is "they must think I'm worth it," to spend money on (tickets to Europe), driving two hours to meet for the first time, buying expensive art, meals, and jewelry, buying a phone so they could be in contact with me all the time (cringe), and the list goes on. I know I'm not alone here.

The big issue here was my self esteem and lack of self love. I was operating in the negative emotionally when it came to relationships because I didn't love myself. I didn't know how to and my past hurts were taking center stage because past hurts that weren't resolved reared their heads and played a part in the new relationship.

Giving yourself away because you don't love yourself or don't know how to love yourself is exactly what I was doing. This was a pattern in my life and it was very apparent when it came to relationships.

Being needy and relying on others to love me and therefore validate me made me feel weak. Why did this keep happening?

Note: Pay attention to your patterns. They keep showing up for a reason and will continue to show up until you've learned what you're supposed to learn.

I don't like feeling weak because feeling weak was somehow associated with me lying on the bed being assaulted when I was a little girl. However, at the time I couldn't understand the correlation between the assault and my relationships as an adult.

Please know that the feeling of being weak was not a conscious thought. It was buried deep in me. It was a sense, more than a knowing. The only way to describe that is that I never had the conscious thought, as some have, "It was my fault." "I was weak." It was never like that. Not once have I ever thought it was my fault.

Which makes it even more fascinating that feeling needy and weak in a relationship was directly related to an assault that took place decades ago. What that says to me is that the emotions and feelings that were not allowed to be played out during the assault were so buried in my body that it took years, many relationships, and countless life experiences to be able to come out.

Let's loop back to my mantra and theme of "I don't do relationships well." Many of my trusted friends and teachers and therapists have since "corrected" me about my "it was me" belief when it comes to being my fault. It wasn't me that was "doing it wrong," it was me looking for external validation that I was worthy. It was my trauma drama bumping into the relationship.

What was really happening from my part of the relationship was that it was little me, the "why did he do that, why would he hurt me?" little girl who had been assaulted and needed validation and healing. She needed to be seen and heard. She needed to have someone care for her hurts, for her pain. She needed a voice and because she wasn't able at the times of the assaults to either fight back or run, she froze and all the feelings and all the negative energy stayed inside. Stuck inside.

When she was not validated, she ran the show internally. She grew up to be a needy teen who grew up feeling like a needy weak young adult – in emotional situations.

The little unhealed me craved love and nurturance. She craved safety and security and when men paid attention to me it felt like I mattered enough to be loved and not harmed. I was valued.

Where did that feeling of being unloved come from? Why did I crave it so desperately? Was it passed down to me from my mom as well? What else was not processed from her past that she passed to me other than money and men? What unresolved emotions did she inherit from her mother, my grandma?

It was also my inability to handle stress well and for my system to regulate. I don't know how my mother handled her stress and I wonder now how my grandma handled (or didn't) her stress. How they processed their cortisol (stress hormone released into our systems when the system is activated).

When I think back to how my grandma's life was as a little girl, I'm in awe that she was as grounded and well put together as she appeared to be. Her life was not easy as a child. She lived during prohibition, had a horrible step mother who verbally assaulted her, had an asshole alcoholic father, lost her mother when she was 10 due to her mother having a miscarriage related to a fall. She was a very good student, loved school, and graduated from eighth grade but was pulled out of school because "she had to work" when she was in ninth grade.

As my grandma, I observed her cook, clean, and sit for hours watching TV. I never questioned it. It was what she did. I often wonder if she was in a freeze state as well and if so how that was passed down in the family. How could she have not been in a freeze state after surviving all of that? How did her unresolved hurt affect my mother and me? Referencing back to the ACE study mentioned before, my grandmother would score very high. Think about that.

TEACHABLE MOMENT

When children are victimized, the hurt stays in the body. We don't feel safe. We don't feel loved. We feel scared. We are afraid and fear stops everything. If we grow up with fear in our bodies it will run the show behind the scenes until it is released. These early ruptures cause lifelong hardships. To paraphrase Bessel Van der Kolk, "we need to feel safe, protected, and strong to heal." How do we do that? We use body based tools in conjunction with other modalities that help us. Having a body based practice is paramount to healing. You cannot talk your way out of trauma. It is in every cell of your being. It is and was also in every cell of those in your family of origin. The body is designed to move. Movement heals. Movement is medicine for fear and movement is freedom. Movement also strengthens the cortex (the rational part of the brain), which then overrides the emotional part of the brain when life happens. It's the emotional part of the brain which takes center stage during stress and trauma. Helping to strengthen the cortex can help decrease the alarm bells and whistles from going off all the time. Learn your family's history. The past teaches us about the present. When we learn how trauma works and when we understand our family history, it can build empathy and help us look at our current life through a different lens.

"…history gives us the tools to analyze and explain problems in the past, it positions us to see patterns that might otherwise be invisible in the present – thus providing a crucial perspective for understanding (and solving!) current and future problems."*

"95% of trauma is multigenerational, that's just how it works. We unwittingly pass it on. Whatever was passed on to you happened through your parents; and through your parents' experience in life which they hadn't quite resolved by the time they had you."
~Gabor Maté
(interview on Mind Body Green)

* https://history.wisc.edu/undergraduate-program/history-careers/why-history/

Uncovering the
Real Hurt & Forgiveness
as a Healing Tool

unhealed wounds

show up

in many ways

A few years ago I was standing in my mom's kitchen with my mom and aunt. It was a family weekend and my aunt and uncle came from Door County and were staying at my mom's house. Mom, Aunt Sandra, and I were talking and my aunt casually commented about the hat I was wearing. One of my favorite hats. I love this hat. I wear it all the time, especially in Wisconsin because half the year we have snow... well almost. Not a huge fan of winter other than to look at it. So, this hat. I love this hat for two reasons.

One, it says (embroidered, no less) "Me Too" on it and was made by one of my favorite people, one of my first yoga teachers, yoga mentor, and overall amazing human being, Monique. She started a clothing line a few years ago and I love her line. Plus, supporting fellow female entrepreneurs is absolutely a win.

As I tell my aunt about Monique and I acknowledge my connection with the "me too" statement, without missing a beat, my mom looks at the hat, reads it, and replies, "Oh honey, yes, but that was a long time ago." In a nanosecond my eyes locked with my aunt's and I could feel the tears coming. She knew. She could sense it. My mom was not aware of how her comment affected me.

I could feel the emotions rushing to the surface, I was going to say bubbling, but there was no way this was bubbling. That would imply that the sensation was subtle. This was not subtle. It was definitely rushing to the surface. Flooding was more like it, if I'm totally honest. Flooding with overwhelming sadness.

I immediately ran to the bathroom, sat on the toilet, and sobbed. I was shocked. I was stunned. I was in disbelief that my mom would say that. What the hell? I went through a litany of "She has no idea still after all these years," "She'll never understand," "What the F---?" and on and on and on. My reaction even startled me a little.

It felt like this hiding in the bathroom lasted forever. In reality it lasted maybe five minutes before I could get my shit together and go back out and have an adult conversation and not act like an overreacting, overemotional adult. By getting my shit together, I mean: wait for the crying to stop, be able to take a full complete deep breath, wipe my face from the snot and tears, and settle down my overactive and critical brain.

Once my brain and body calmed down I was able to go back to the kitchen and visit. My aunt knew I'd been crying; it's hard to hide red puffy eyes. My mother never said a word.

I was still shocked, but for a different reason. Not that my mom had no idea how I felt or went through and realistically never will (how could she... right?), or would even say such a thing, but that I had such an over-the-top reaction to her statement. That's the clencher here.

Why? Because I can talk to almost anyone about the assault. I can share with friends, with clients, students (when appropriate), and with mass audiences, but when it comes to my mother, who was supposed to be there for me, to protect me, in reality she wasn't there when any of these shitty things happened to me. It wasn't as if she knew. She had no idea this shit was going on. She was somewhere else.

Don't get me wrong. I'm not throwing my mother under the bus. Not even a little.... well... maybe a little. I believe keeping your children safe is in the unwritten and highly controversial mom contract somewhere in the large print at the top. Or at least in the middle before the small print at the bottom that talks about feeding and clothing and taking temperatures and driving to all the things and paying for all the things and more.

As Kelly McDaniel, author of *Mother Hunger* puts it, she describes "mothering" as requiring three essential elements: nurturance, protection, and guidance. As a child I didn't feel protected during and after this happened, which then led to me constantly feeling "anxious and afraid."

The reason I have to forgive my mother is that there is no way she could have known. How could she? Unless I told her. Which I did not until many years later.

My mother was a teacher and an administrator. She was a gifted teacher with an enormous heart. She went out of her way to support and help her students. This amazing skill transferred to her volunteer work for a political party after she retired. She still volunteers at 81 years old. She is amazing.

Regardless, I didn't tell… I didn't tell my mother or any other adult for almost eight years. I did tell two friends. I had no words for what happened. There was no memory bank of what to do with this. Sex or anything sexual was not part of my world at that age.

Another reason (deeply buried subconscious reason) I didn't tell her at the time was at some level scared of him. I was afraid of him because, after one of the assaults, as he walked out of the room, he looked at me with a threatening look. No words were needed. I got the message. I stayed frozen in bed for a long while after that.

I now understand from therapy and years of working in the mental health field, and studying and teaching about trauma, that, yes, the assaults were scary. However, my system responded the way it was designed to. It kept me safe by lying there and not fighting or trying to run. By basically playing dead, I (my body) was safer that way and my mind could escape (dissociate) until it was over.

The other reality of this is that little me was more upset at my mom for not being there to protect me, to make it stop, to keep me safe, than I was at him for actually assaulting me. I was afraid of him. I was mad at her. It made perfect sense to me when my therapist brought up that idea and we dissected it.

The other side of this coin is that we as a society generally do not understand how stress and trauma work unless you work in a field that requires you to do so. And unless you have a framework of how to handle this type of experience you may not handle it so well if you try to unpack it at all.

There is no way my mother could have known what to do when I told her other than what she did by calling her attorney. She's a brilliant problem solver. She responded with her brilliant brain. But she wasn't, however, equipped to help me navigate the yuck (the emotional baggage) that comes with childhood sexual assault.

I absolutely needed a champion in my court who believed me, who did all the things in the background that needed to be done.

What I needed that I did not get, though, was nurturance. I needed to be held and hugged and consoled, regardless of how old I was when the story came out. I needed to be able to cry until the tears stopped. To be told I would be ok. That she was sorry she was not there to protect me. That she was sorry he hurt me and that she would protect me. Why? Because little me, her little Christy, was still holding on to a lot of pain and I carried this pain with me wherever I went like a 200 pound weighted vest. This vest is the anxiety that makes taking a deep breath hard. That makes trust hard. That makes other interpersonal relationships hard. That makes me feel like I'm weighted down at times and can't do anything.

That's also my depression. My unprocessed emotions. Why I get migraines. Why relationships can be hard at times because expectations of unmet needs are lurking in the shadows waiting to be acknowledged and heard.

Forgiveness

Forgiving my mom for not doing what I needed her to do, when she didn't know it needed to be done, is part of the process. It's acceptance that it was what it was. At the time of the assaults she was elsewhere. She trusted him to be a responsible adult and that didn't go as planned. Neither does life if we're being realistic. If life was easy, we would not have the amazing "a ha" moments that we get. I'm not suggesting that I'd wish for this by any means, but it did make me the person I am today.

I believe it's made me more compassionate. It's made me a great mom. It's helped me be able to hold space for women who have struggled with similar issues and understand what they are going through... we often just need someone to listen. It's made me a champion for people who need the playing field leveled. It's given me the passion for movement and the need to share the power of movement with everyone I meet. It's given me the drive to understand how trauma works and then share it with others. It's also provided the framework for me to cultivate a daily self care and stress management routine that has many times saved me from driving over the proverbial cliff. It made me self sufficient. I'm sure there is more...

So forgiving my mother for not being there is, yes, part of the work, but it was also part of the bigger picture of loving people for who they are. Not who we want them to be.

It's also the classic saying, "She did the best she could with what she had." Just as I have done... and if we can be happy with 80% of what we have... I'll take it. Think of it as the Pareto Rule (80/20) for living and loving people. None of us always get it right. Nothing is 100% when it comes to people. We are messy. We are complicated. We are also amazing. I'll take 80% of the magic and leave the 20% to the other.

I've said many times over the last few years (in relation to myself and to my clients who struggle with Mother Hunger) that we are given the mother that we need. Not necessarily the mother we want. Would I have liked some things to be different? Of course. But if my mother were a completely different person I would not be the me I am today. And I'm pretty damn proud of who I am today and the lessons I've learned from my stories: surviving college and graduating with honors, successfully single parenting, and more.

The other part of forgiveness is forgiving myself. Forgiving myself for not knowing. Forgiving myself for being an asshole at times because I was overloaded and overwhelmed and just over it. Forgiving myself for not being the perfect mom. For saying dumb things. For not always being available and any other faux pas or ripples in the family fabric that I caused.

The flip side of this when your intention is to be a cycle breaker is to not get caught up in the "what if" part. We could "what if" ourselves to death. Not healthy. Learn. Grow. Accept. Forgive. Do Better. Having an awareness without attachment is the idea.

The forgiveness part is the acceptance of a bigger picture. It's forgiving my mom for being human and accepting all of her just as she is. It's forgiving myself for the things I need to forgive myself for. It's also part of the puzzle that is me, because everything is connected. Trauma segments us not only from ourselves but also from others. Forgiveness is part of the healing equation that brings us and those we love back to wholeness.

THE AHA MOMENT... IT'S ALL CONNECTED

When I was going through the divorce with my girls' father, as I mentioned earlier, I went to therapy. What I learned this time in therapy was not necessarily what I went to see her for. Surprise!!!

I thought I was there to help me process my divorce. To help me understand why I was so miserable. To understand what happened and to process the pain and hurtful things said to me. So I could understand and heal.

What actually came out of those sessions, other than reading a book on "Crazy Making" and the correlation to my marriage ending, was that I learned that little me blamed my mother for the sexual assault from over 30 years ago because she wasn't there to protect me. WAIT, WHAT? I blamed her? What? Yes, I blamed her. It was subconscious, but little me blamed her. Not adult me. Little me.

Why would I blame my mother? She wasn't there. That's not only a ridiculous thought but a horrible one. Well not really as I learned and here's why.

Little me, six-to-eight-year-old me, needed to try and make sense of why it happened and why I always felt bad. Why I was sad, shy (in certain circles), felt uncomfortable in my skin, was full of self loathing and self doubt, isolated, and the list goes on forever.

I had no idea what sex was, had no experience with it, never heard of it or been exposed to it, my brain basically said, "what is this, why are you doing this, it hurts, I don't like it, make it stop, momma why aren't you making him stop?" Of course these "thoughts" were not conscious nor did I ever say them out loud. I do very clearly remember the "it hurts" part though.

The connection between me trying to process and heal from my divorce and process and heal the childhood assault are directly related. My unresolved childhood pain and need for healing were showing up in adult me.

Little me didn't heal or get the validation that she needed. As a matter of fact, with the court case being dismissed it was the opposite, as was it when Rick's attorney told me I made it up to hurt him. The dismissal, denial, and accusation put an entirely different cloud around the pain. Little me felt adults were "supposed to" protect you, love you, not cause pain and then blame you for it.

What adult me needed at that time was help and support and I also needed validation that I wasn't crazy. My higher self knew that I wasn't crazy.

When I understood the correlation between the pain of my marriage, the fact that I needed emotional validation and to heal was directly related to the pain of little hurt me needing emotional validation and to heal, I was shocked but I understood.

They both were painful situations. They both hurt me emotionally. Neither time did I feel validated that the hurt actually happened. In both situations I was blamed. Neither time did I get the emotional support I needed that someone who was "supposed to love me" actually hurt me.

Which is exactly how little me felt subconsciously. I blamed my mom for not protecting me (which on a logical level makes sense, right?). She was supposed to love me and keep me safe and she didn't.

Once I understood this, I mean really understood this, I felt great and relieved that I had this huge insight, it was a relief because I could never make sense of why I needed so desperately to be validated and loved. It also made sense why I'd always had a slight undertow of being mad at my mom. It went back to her. The relief I felt having this "a ha" moment was brilliant. I felt like that proverbial weight had been lifted and I couldn't wait to share it with her.

I was nervous because I wasn't sure how she'd respond.

How would you respond if your child told you that she felt you were responsible, partly, for her pain. Let me tell you... If you're not in a good place or solid in your being, you might be emotionally knocked over or any other litany of negative emotions.

There was an interesting emotional dance that was going on in my head when I thought about telling her. Little me was scared she'd get mad and react or yell. My adult brain hoped she'd take it well and understand.

I did tell her. I told her immediately after getting out of the car from the appointment. I braced for impact. I told her what the therapist concluded. She listened and said, "Oh, honey that makes so much sense. I'm so sorry."

I was proud of myself for telling her. I was elated and my body felt like it exhaled for the first time in 30 some years. Had I let my anxiety take over I would have never told her. Take away... bravery wins. Things change. We are stronger than we think. If we survived shit in our childhood and we're here showing up for ourselves, THAT IS A WIN!

TEACHABLE MOMENT

Understanding how deeply this pain was buried and how many tendrils it had allowed me to see the bigger picture. It allowed me to see my story in a different light. It allowed me to zoom out and see how it was little me who subconsciously blamed my mother for the hurt I was experiencing. It also allowed me to be able to dissect all the parts of how one person's actions have a direct and an indirect impact on so many. It allowed me to be able to begin the work of forgiving my mother when I didn't know it was her who I was holding to blame for what he did. It also gave me a deeper understanding of the layers of healing that had to happen in order for the deeper one to be exposed. It took my divorce from my girls' father and seeking help to unravel that to bring the next layer down to the surface. The proverbial lotus flower. This is the wisdom of my trauma(s). It's given me the agency to want to change the legacy in my family.

The Story

Brace for impact here if this stuff makes you uncomfortable. I won't get too graphic, but still want to paint a subtly graphic picture of what happened.

Keep in mind sexual assault comes in many different shapes and sizes. This book shares what happened to me, how it affected me, lessons I learned along the way, and how I handle it now as a 50-something, intelligent, fun, beautiful, well educated woman who just happens to swear a lot and likes to laugh.

Disclaimer:

If you and I ever have the amazing opportunity to meet in person or you hear me speak at an event, you may notice some small inconsistencies in my story. Not what happened, but the small details as I paint the picture. Why? Because that's what stress and trauma do to the brain. Generally speaking they make things fuzzy.

What happened? There were a few different times he, Rick Wilson, the man who adopted me when he married my mom, messed with me, for lack of a better term. My biological father was never part of the picture.

Two times he had his hands inside me and the other two times were just weird sexual predator garbage behavior. The two times he had his hands inside me were nights when he was at our house and my mom was gone.

During the two major events, Rick waited for my mom to be gone during the evening. The other times he did not live with us when the assaults took place. He and my mom were separated and he was at our house taking care of Kevin and me when my mom was working or doing other mom things.

He's passed now. He was a pedofile, he was a sexual predator, he was a womanizer, he was a liar, he was a cheat, and he hurt many people in his lifetime, including my mom.

I know I'm not the only one he sexually assaulted or harassed. There were various charges against him from his female university students over the years.

He was also my brother's father, which complicated things… just a little. My brother, Kevin, and I have two different fathers. My father was my mom's first husband and Kevin's father was her second. Kevin and I grew up together. There's no "half" anything, never has been. He's my baby brother.

But, when it was time for this story to come out it complicated his life. I don't want to speak for him, but I remember very clearly that his father would work ridiculously hard to convince Kevin that it never happened. So much so that he asked Kevin to talk to me about it (even on his deathbed). He is five and a half years younger than me. So when my story came out he was roughly 10.

The other side of Rick is that he was academically brilliant. He was a (Fulbright Professor of Political Science) and a politician. However, being brilliant does not necessarily equate to having Emotional or Social Intelligence (ability to appraise and assess your emotions and others). He had no boundaries... clearly, or reality that suggested to him that trying to involve his 10 year old son in any way was appropriate. Shocking...

I cannot imagine how hard that was for Kevin to get roped into this traumatic event. He also was not emotionally or developmentally prepared to be able to process this story. I always thought of myself as his protector for some reason and I was beyond furious with his father that he attempted to involve him in the story. I've always wished I could take away the confusion, the frustration, and the anger that he may have felt. He was just a little boy.

The first time it happened, he came into my room after I was asleep, woke me up and made some comment about me not being able to sleep and he wanted to "help me sleep." Yes, weird and creepy, I agree. None of us (family and legal team) are positive how old I was exactly but it was in the eight to ten age range... I was young.

He said he would help by "rubbing my legs." He then had me (not sure how, but he had the control) lie on my stomach and he began to rub the back of my legs.

For those of you wondering if writing about this is emotional... it is. I've cried (healing tears) a few times as I write these stories and I appreciate it when this happens. Why? Because just when you think you've learned that lesson or healed from that thing, it shows up again out of nowhere... lovely and thanks for having my back, universe.

It's also good for me. Crying is healthy and healing. We don't allow ourselves enough time for this...

Back to little eight-to-ten-year-old me, in my bedroom. It was night time. It was dark and he was rubbing the back of my legs. I vaguely remember him asking me something but I have no idea what it was. I just remember it going on forever.

At some point he began to open my legs wider and rub higher and harder. He continued this pattern. His moving my legs wider was subtle. I remember feeling really uncomfortable, but also having no idea what he was doing or what he was going to do. I didn't know what to do. I must have faked being asleep because I believe he thought I was and that's when he made his move.

He started to put his fingers (or something) inside me. I assume it was his fingers since I didn't have the sense he was physically on top of me. My bed was situated in the room so the head of the bed was against a wall and window with an air conditioner. Yes, the window style ones. While he did his thing, I focused on the noise of the air conditioner. It hurt a lot and he did it for what seemed forever.

I don't remember anything after that or even the next day, but I remember it happened again. I also don't remember the time in between both events.

Same situation, different day. He was at the house. My mom was gone. This time I was sleeping in a bedroom downstairs. Not my bedroom that was upstairs. Once again he did exactly what he'd done before. Came in. Woke me up and said he'd help me get to sleep.

Eight-to-ten-year-old me didn't have the skills, tools, or knowledge or anything that equipped me to tell him to stop. So it happened again.

Let's be very very very clear here. I'm going to rant a little. Because people will say (not you reading this, you're amazing, but others as they historically have), "why didn't you stop it? Regardless of what age you could have stopped it."

NO, YOU CAN'T. I couldn't. I was a child. He was the adult. Little me was terrified and so I froze and fawned… My system did what it needed to do to protect me.

When you're an adult and experience sexual abuse, you MAY or MAY NOT have developed the skills to fight off an abuser.

Or you also may have developed resilience as an adult and have a more mature developed brain that helps cope in the aftermath of the yuck. OR maybe you didn't.

Regardless, it doesn't matter if you have these protection skills or not. What matters is there have historically been and will continue to be... beings behaving badly. Causing harm to others. Sexally assaulting/abusing others.

We know this, we see it in the media and social media all the time. Or we hear of it through the grapevine. I hear it from my clients all the time. It's awful. It sucks and it happens. What can you do? We'll get into that later. Keep reading...

The current statistics of women within the U.S. being sexually assaulted is one in six, according to RAINN (Rape, Abuse, and Incest National Network) the nation's largest anti-sexual violence organization.*

- Every 9 minutes Child Protective Services substantiates or finds evidence for, or a claim for child sexual abuse

- In 2016 alone, Child Protective Services agencies substantiated, or found strong evidence to indicate that, 57,329 children were victims of sexual abuse

- 1 out of every 6 American women has been the victim of an attempted or completed rape in her lifetime (14.8% completed, 2.8% attempted)

- 1 in 9 girls and 1 in 53 boys under the age of 18 experience sexual abuse or assault at the hands of an adult

- 82% of all victims under 18 are female

- Females ages 16-19 are 4 times more likely than the general population to be victims of rape, attempted rape, or sexual assault

- Out of every 1,000 sexual assaults, 310 are reported to the police

These stats are only a *partial* snapshot of what's actually happening in the United States due to the numbers who report. And these numbers are old, from 2016. Why? Because research and collecting and reporting on data (statistics) takes forever. Can you imagine this job?!

* https://www.rainn.org/statistics/children-and-teens

There's also a reason why women DON'T REPORT. I'll share my experience with that, too.

Back to the lovely details.

This time was different though in that I figured I knew what he was planning to do. I was pretty sure. He once again had me lie on my stomach and began rubbing my legs. This time though, when he tried to move them open wider, I clenched. I tried to resist. That backfired because he then slowly forced them open. I remember sensing (again not knowing, because my rational eight-to-ten-year-old brain was offline at this time… it was trying to fight, but I couldn't so I froze and or fawned ("people please," to stay safe).

He continued to pry my legs open and then did what he did last time. He put his hands inside me and repeated this in and out motion until he was through. I didn't realize until recently (ha, funny how the mind works) what else he was probably doing.

It hurt like hell, just like the last time. I tuned out this time into a space heater that was on the nightstand. I can still see the orange thin lines if I think about it. You know those old ones that were metal and had heated wires that turned orange when it was turned on?

When he was done, this is where I got scared. (I obviously wasn't asleep, either time though I pretended to be.) He got up and as he was walking out of the room, I turned my head and looked at him. He looked back at me with a look that to me said, "if you tell, you're done," or something lovely like that. That actually scared me far more than what he'd just done. I felt like he was threatening me without actually saying anything.

The other two times or things he did (keep in mind I have no idea in what order or when these things happened… but I do remember weather/temperature details so that gives me a hint as to what time of year) were different in nature and less physically painful, but still creepy and scary to little me.

I have a vague memory of him being at home with me either alone or with my little brother Kevin while my mom was gone. Regardless, he was "the adult" at home. I don't know what was going on, but he picked me up, threw me over his shoulders as one does to carry a child around, and walked around what I think was the dining room in our house. Normal behavior? Yes, possibly. But not the way he did it.

He picked me up so I was upside down but facing away from him. He put my legs over his shoulders and my crotch right in his face. I remember him sniffing, because I could hear it and feel it. It lasted only a moment, but the effect it had felt like it lasted a lot longer. Something in me sensed, or knew, that it was not right.

The other lovely situation he created involved more details and a story. I'm setting it up that way, because he had to put some extra thought into it (like he didn't before… right) but this was different. It felt different.

I know... the suspense is killing you.

Humor and brevity, right?

To set the stage... it was a weekend, again my mom was gone. We must have been cleaning windows or screens or something because I remember our backyard being full of windows or screens resting against the countless trees in our backyard. It looked like a cemetery for windows. Big white wooden rectangular frames resting on the sides of brown skinny tree trunks. It seemed like they were endless when in reality it was probably a dozen or so... but I was little.

I was across the street at a neighbor's house with the boys. I was the only girl on my block. I lived across from four boys. Two sets of brothers; each with one older, close to my age and two younger. I was friends with two of the brothers and hung out at their house all the time. There was also a boy who was part of the friend group, but he lived a block or two away. So five boys total and me.

We were in the garage of the two brothers who I didn't spend much time with. I'm not sure why we were in the garage other than a vague memory of planning to go in the house through the inside garage door. I'd only ever been in this house once or twice.

So what happened next is foggy at best, because it was still odd that I was in the garage with the other boys as I usually wasn't invited to hang out with this set of brothers or be in their house. Hmmmm...

Before I knew it, the oldest pulled my pants down. They all laughed. I froze and was humiliated and scared… why would my so-called friends do this? I'm pretty sure the two brothers I was closer with had no idea this was going to happen. They weren't ever mean to me and we spent a lot of time together.

I have no idea how or when I pulled my pants up or even how I got home (across the street), but I did.

It gets better…

Once I'm at home, step-father Rick can clearly tell something is wrong. He asks me about it. I tell him and start crying.

This lovely human then decides that this is a good time to tell me about STDs. I'd never heard of STDs. Let me paint a picture so you can really get the juicy details… don't worry this isn't horrific, just creepy.

He must have asked me to sit down and tell him the story because I vividly remember him sitting on our brown leather couch in his reeeeeeaaaaaaalllllly short cut off khaki green shorts and me sitting in a chair across from him in our TV room, just off the kitchen. It was sort of a great room that was at the back of the house so I could see the window graveyard by looking straight ahead.

He asked me what happened. I told him. He made some comment about John (the boy who pulled my pants down) and then started talking about STDs and what "happens to boys."

What? Seriously? Yes, Seriously. You guessed it. He started to describe erections and how they happen.

As he's telling me… it was like he was speaking a foreign language to me because kissing a boy then wasn't even in my vernacular. As he's telling me… he gets an erection. He then gets up, walks towards me, as he's still talking and then pulls out one of his testicles (he reached up and pulled it out from near the inseam). It was hard, hairy, and DISGUSTING. Remember I was young. Of course it was disgusting.

He then made me touch it. How did he make me? I was scared of what he'd do if I didn't do as I was told. I must have hesitated…

He's standing next to me, holding one of his balls, talking about STDs and whatever other ridiculous and inappropriate topics he was talking about and asks me to touch it to demonstrate "what happens to boys."

I must have said no, because he then took my hand and made me touch him. I remember feeling sick to my stomach. It was nasty. I can feel my teeth and jaw starting to clench as I write this.

I froze again and don't remember much after that.

I think he just went on with his day.

To the best of my knowledge, those four stories are what I remember. I say "what I remember" because I now, some 50 years later, have an intimate understanding of how our stress and trauma system works; how I responded to what was happening to me from a neuro-physiological place. Especially childhood trauma and how the body's internal safety systems kick in to keep us safe; which includes the rational part of the brain, the prefrontal cortex (the newest part of the brain), going offline. Meaning it shuts down so one of the other parts of the brain responsible for keeping us safe can take over and prep us for fight or flight (or freeze, flood, dissociate, and/or fawn).

The stairs - Finding my power, fighting back, a little
Sometime during the years that Rick was "messing with me," he was once again at our house to take care of Kevin and me. Again, foggy memory, but it was during the day. Mom was away and he came over with food in plastic containers. I remember the containers in vivid detail because back in the 70s, the plastic industry hadn't taken over the planet so we didn't have cupboards full of plastic containers with matching lids that we bought from Sam's Club or some other big box store.

At our house, we used empty margarine containers for leftovers that were pretty heavy duty brightly colored plastic bowls. They were blue, yellow, orange, lime green and some other colors. You can still find them on ebay or etsy now and buy them as collectibles. How funny!

The reason the food containers are such a big deal is that Rick thought it was a huge deal that he brought food over for us and was very irritated at me that I didn't want to eat the food he brought.

The colors are important here because for a good portion of my life it felt like I was living in black and white. I'm not color blind, that's not it. I love color and live in and use color intentionally now, but when I think back on significant times in my life, I don't remember color much, which I think is really interesting given that stress and trauma make us myopic (narrow in thinking) and it can feel like living in black and white.

I remember one bowl had sliced roast beef in it, nasty and not a fan. I don't remember the others. The point is, he got upset with me for not wanting to "eat his food." He said that to me.

The next thing that happened was really interesting because it started what I call an energetic and verbal power struggle that felt very weird for me. I don't remember having the feeling or thoughts that I would fight back if he tried something, I just remember I knew something could possibly happen, based on history and whatever it was he wanted me to do or wanted to do to me I was not going to put up with it… and that included eating his shitty leftovers.

Once he knew I wasn't going to eat his food, he began to elevate, meaning he began to posture and changed from a "here look what I did for you" (brought food) nice guy mode to someone who was being challenged. He couldn't understand that I was pushing back. I was resisting whatever he had in mind, regardless of what it was. I remember sensing (I say sensing because I don't remember actually having specific thoughts like: he's here, he might try to mess with me again, I'm not going to let that happen and maybe more) that he wasn't going to force me to do anything I didn't want to do.

Now here's where it gets interesting. I don't remember these as thoughts. Meaning they weren't things I said in my head to myself. It was more something I sensed and I knew I was going to push back and not tolerate any bullshit... it's hard to explain because it wasn't conscious.

Was it subconscious? It was almost as if I was being directed by something else. I was part of a play and I was the actor. It was an inner knowing what I had to do. Believe me, at that age, challenging an adult was not something I ever thought was a thing. I was taught or at least it was implied to respect adults.

Regardless, he got angry with me after I refused to eat his food. I then ran towards the staircase that led to my bedroom on the second floor. I do remember being scared. I was hiding and not visible to the rest of the house if he were looking for me because in order for him to see me he had to turn a corner to get to the stairs from the living room. I wasn't visible unless he planned to climb the stairs so I sat there... hiding and waiting.

This type of cat and mouse game was not something that had ever happened to me before. I wasn't sure what to do so I just sat there and waited, hoping he would leave me alone. He didn't.

I must have been able to hear him, because I remember moving up the stairs backwards on my butt. I didn't turn and run. I had to be able to see. I had to be able to see what was coming so I wasn't caught off guard or surprised as I was when he came into the rooms I was sleeping in before. I had to be facing him to be able to fight him off if he tried something.

Again these weren't thoughts. I knew this is what I had to do. I was probably halfway up the stairs when he appeared. He slowly started to come up the stairs while asking/insisting that I come down and eat. I refused and each time he took a step up the stairs, I backed up a step.

I remember telling him to stop multiple times. I told him if he continued to come towards me I would scream. He kept coming slowly towards me.

Eventually I was at the top step and remembered having the sense that I couldn't go any farther. Almost as if my body was frozen in place.

If I remember correctly (remember... stress chemicals cloud the brain so my memory of this at this point is really fuzzy) it appeared to me that he wasn't going to stop coming up the stairs towards me, so I screamed as loud as I could.

I think I threatened him too.

He must have stopped because I don't remember him coming up to the top.

I also don't remember what happened after that which tells me it was uneventful. Nothing big, hairy, or scary happened. Thank god!

I really don't know why or what happened to me that allowed me to gain strength and stand up to him. To stand in my power… even as a little girl. But I did and I'm grateful the story ended there.

He made no more attempts to touch me. To expose himself to me. To do weird things to me. It just stopped. If I did threaten him… it worked.

At least the abuse stopped. The story continued in the form of me carrying it around in my being for years and then it came out in the fury to my mom.

It stays with you. Like a festering wound deep inside. Until it doesn't.

The hard thing about having these experiences, memories, and stories, is that they are all cloudy. They're fuzzy at best. Which from a rational adult standpoint makes them almost hard to believe. But when you've lived these experiences… you have these stories in your body. You have them in your bones. You know.

It's recalling the specific details, the subtle nuances of how things happened, who said what, the sequence of events, the color of things around you, the sites, the smells, the sounds, they all get fuzzy. It's like physically being a part or playing a role in something really shitty that's happening to you. Knowing it's happening because you sense it, you're part of the experience, but it's like a slow motion, vague, fuzzy, black and white dream.

I know why. I now know as an adult, who's studied how the brain and body respond to trauma, why this happens. But knowing how and why something works the way it does and having the experiences in your body like a blueprint so solid that it's become part of your structure, while having the brain only vaguely remember the specifics is odd.

But that's how it works. This is why I believe it is paramount that we understand how trauma works on a whole person brain-body level. I believe we no longer have the luxury of not knowing.

In the last few years there have been a few stories made public or brought to light by many brave survivors who share their story. One in particular in 2018 was the widely public case between Supreme Court nominee Brett Kavanaugh and Dr. Christine Blasey Ford, that debated a sexual assault that took place decades prior.

Lady Gaga, when asked about the case on the Stephen Colbert Show in reference to "the validity of the memories of Dr. Ford," stated, "there is science that supports this" and "someone who experiences sexual assault takes the trauma and puts it in a box and files it away and shuts it so that we can survive the pain."

She added, "it also does a lot of other things. It can cause body pain, it can cause, you know, baseline elevations in anxiety. It can cause complete avoidance of wanting to even remember or think about what happened to you." Gaga said she believes that when Ford saw that Kavanaugh was selected as a Supreme Court nominee, "that box opened, she was brave enough to share it with the world to protect this country."**

I add this here because there is bravery demonstrated when women share their stories publicly. It gives a voice, validation, and power to not only the woman sharing her story but also the countless others who cannot. Both Dr. Ford and Lady Gaga are each in a powerful position that allows them to have the public's ear.

The stress of publicly sharing your story alone can be damning. Especially when discredit and shame is the name of the game (or worse) and the science behind stress and trauma is not brought to the forefront because it's still a relatively new science or only shared between a therapist and their client or as professional development for those in the mental health fields. Earlier I explained how the stress response system works. Understanding brings power. Pay attention…

Dr. Dan Seigel's "Flipping Your Lid" Theory helps explain with brilliant technique how our brain works

** https://www.cbsnews.com/news/lady-gaga-late-show-with-stephen-colbert-sexual-assault-survivor-brett-kavanaugh-christine-blasey-ford/

during stressful and traumatic events. During normal life experiences the parts of the brain function as one whole unit. However, during stressful experiences the frontal lobes of the **cortex (newest part of the brain)** are inhibited by the activation of the **limbic system** and **brain stem (older parts responsible for survival)**. The cortex goes offline and lets the other parts do the work to keep us safe.

The purpose of this neurological separation is so that executive functioning (rational thinking, problem solving, planning, organizing, and more) is out of the way so our instinctual survival responses can be activated. It's brilliant. The Limbic system is the part of the brain involved when it comes to behaviors we need for survival: feeding, reproduction, and caring for our young, and regulates our fight or flight responses.

Part of this internal safety system is the autonomic nervous system which is always scanning our environment to determine if we are safe. This scanning happens without our knowing by evaluating our environment for "cues of safety". This scanning of our environment is a term developed by Dr. Stephen Porges called neuroception.

Dr. Porges, who I introduced on page 56, work is widely recognized in the field of trauma and helps explain what goes on behind the scenes (our autonomic nervous system), how our emotional states are affected by stress and trauma, how our systems communicate with one another, and how by better understanding what goes on behind the scenes we can better understand and support ourselves and others.

What is known about trauma and what it does to the brain is becoming more widely known with research and mental health awareness. We still have a long way to go before it's known and understood by the masses.

Bravo to the brave women who have put themselves on the public stage to shed light on this for the masses.

Children who experience trauma, whose brain is still developing, can have their brain hijacked. When we completely understand this, it can help explain a lot of behavior. If you are a child who is carrying unprocessed stress and traumatic memories in your body, coupled with everyday stressors, the switch into "primitive behaviors" goes off often. Think about our current increase in autoimmune diseases in women and children, just for a start.

"It isn't what's wrong with you...
It is what happened to you."
-Oprah Winfrey

I love this quote, because "What's wrong with you?" was said to me only once in my life by an adult when I was a 20-something. Those words became buried in my bones because they resonated with my fear.

well that didn't turn out well...

My Dad Story
Feeling Unwhole

For most of my life, until I was close to 30ish, my mom had done a magical job of never slamming my father, my birth father.

He was not part of the picture at all. He and my mom ended their marriage before I was born. It was fast, furious, and very short lived from what I've been told. She was a 20-something from the midwest, who was part of a Macalester College and The Hilton Hotels International work abroad program. She'd gone to Athens (Greece) to work for a summer at the Athens Hilton. They met there. She was placed in housekeeping which is also the department he worked in.

He was Greek. She was German and Danish and from the Midwest. Interesting combo to say the least.

I don't know much about the story other than his mother warned my mom by using a hand gesture (made a stabbing motion in the air with a knife because my mom spoke no Greek), that my dad could be dangerous or violent.

The short story goes that my YiaYia (Greek for grandma) picked up a knife that was sitting on a bed and made stabbing motions and said "Rico Rico no no."

To this day my mom and I still don't know exactly what she meant, but the inference was there. "He could cause pain."

Apparently they'd dated long distance for a year. Whatever long distance dating was pre-internet. He asked her to come back. She went back.

They got married... a no no for a Midwest girl in the 1960s. They took a ship and other means to get to the States and he hurt her on the way.

They landed in St. Paul, Minnesota, where Mom had lived and went to college at Macalester University. I can only imagine what it was like for him moving from Athens, Greece, to St. Paul, Minnesota, in the 60s.

No culture shock at all.

The weather is exactly the same...

The food is exactly the same...

The... is the same...

You get my point.

Again, as I've said before, I'm not giving him a pass for being an ass. But knowing the whole story, meaning the back story for context, can be helpful.

I'm pretty convinced, based on pictures that I now have of him as a young adult, posing in front of a pyramid in Egypt and acting like he thinks he's James Dean (60s Hollywood heartthrob), that when he landed here it was the polar opposite of what he thought he was getting when he married my mom. They ended up in St. Paul because Mom easily got a job at Macalester and they needed money to live. My father spoke five languages and very quickly got a job at the Hotel St. Paul. After a month or so he was sought after and hired by a business that made skis and sold them to French speaking Canadians.

Without going into all the details of how fun it was for her, kidding, he did hurt her. He did hit her. He did lock her out of the house in her nightgown in the winter when she was pregnant with me. He did not want me. He told her that. Yup... The marriage ended. Thank god!

As my mom says, "I'd never experienced someone hitting someone else. We didn't do that in our family." And, "we were married long enough for me to have you."

Hmmmm....

To loop back to the beginning of this "dad" story, even with everything he did to her, she never threw him under the proverbial bus. Not once. Not ever. She never said a bad word about him my entire life.

What she did say was, "If you ever want to know about him I'll tell you." That was it. How amazing is that? A lot of women aren't strong enough to keep that pain from their children or have the capacity to be able to understand how potentially damaging it can be for children to hear that their "other" parent was an asshole who hurt people.

She offered off and on my entire life. I never was interested. No idea why, but I wasn't interested. Until I was.

This was how I started being interested in knowing more and actually trying to find him.

Sometime in 1990-something, my mom, her best friend Amy, and Amy's daughter Christie Michele, and I (they distinguished us by calling me Christy Ann) went on a girls trip to Washington, DC.

Amy and Christie are family. Mom and Amy worked together and had been joined at the hip for years. We did a lot of things together and Mom is Christie's and her brother Nathan's God-Mother.

We're in Washington and Amy says as we're touring the Vietnam Wall, "What if he (my dad) was in the Vietnam War and died and left you a lot of money?" Or something like that. We all laughed. We also had no idea where he was at or if he was even alive. My mom had no contact with him after I was born so this was 20 plus years later.

We looked at the names on the wall to see if he was listed there. We looked in the book of other names to see if he was listed there.

No to both.

Oh well, is what I thought. We laughed and that was the end.

Not really.

Amy was at that time dating a man who was into genealogy. This is way before ancestry.com and others were a thing. Because the three of them (Mom, Amy, and Amy's boyfriend) spent a lot of time together, he offered to help me.

"If Christy wants to find her dad let me know and I'll help." Was the phrase I remember hearing. I'd usually say no. But this time was different and I have no idea why.

It was June of 1990-something and it was Father's Day weekend. I was leaving for the night to go to Madison to spend the night at my college roommate's house for a party.

I remember getting in the car and saying to my mom, "Tell (boyfriend's name here) if he wants to try and find my dad, go ahead."

I left. I drove to Madison. I spent the night. We had a massive amount of fun. Drank way too much of course. I spent the night. I drove home.

Here's where the fun starts!

When I got home, this was the chain of events that changed my life forever.

I checked messages on my answering machine (you know those old things that had a blinking light and looked like a tape recorder that used to take voicemails for us before voicemail was a thing).

I listened to the messages.

The only one I heard, no idea if there were others, was my mom saying, "The minute you hear this don't do anything, don't unpack, don't do anything, just come over here immediately, I have news."

Imagine hearing that. Remember... no cell phones then. Uh huh...

So I did. I drove over to her house. No one was on the main level. They were all in the basement. Yes... they. My mom. Her husband. His two children. His son says to me immediately, "Well your Christmas list just got bigger."

What?

And it begins...

My mom begins to tell me what happened in the last 24-48 hours since I left. She gave Amy's friend permission to look up my father and see what he could find. He did and then shared what he found.

He found two individuals with my fathers last name, Varnavas (weird because there is no way that there were only two Varnavas' in the U.S., but oh well). Both men. One was in New York. The other was in a town less than 30 minutes from where my mom and I were born and grew up. The nearby one also had a French first name.

She then located a phone number and called the one close to her hometown in Minnesota.

Mom says she "put two and two together" and it made sense that...

- the one with the "French name" could be Dad's son, because my dad was raised in Egypt in a French Speaking school

- it made sense because Dad had a "friendship" with a waitress at a restaurant in St. Paul that he introduced mom to

- the address provided and phone number prefix given, were from the same town that the waitress was from

Mom made the call.

A woman answered. My mother asked, "Do you know Henri Varnavas?" The woman immediately asked if she was me. My mother explained who she was and that she was calling on my behalf and attempting to locate my father.

The woman shared that she was the mother of the person who she was calling about. My brother. That she was previously married to my father. That she knew who both my mother and I are. That my father was in fact still alive. He was living in San Diego. He was looking for me, too. He was dying of cancer and a very private man.

Holy shit! What?

There were more details, but you get the picture. It was a lot. It was huge. It was... I don't even know what it was, but it was massive. I wouldn't really know until many years later how massive it would become.

From that point (June) until Christmas, I began a letter writing and photo sending and receiving relationship with my father. I also met my brother who I had no idea existed.

The first time my father and I spoke on the phone was one of the most surreal things I'd ever experienced. We scheduled a call. We talked for 30 minutes. I then went to teach aerobics at the gym and was vibrating so much I couldn't even speak clearly.

One of my girlfriends who knew what was going on met me in the backroom as I was trying to get my mic on and saw what a wreck I was and told me to go home, she'd cover my class... thanks, Lisa!

The next few months, as I said, were a blur. It was also amazing, weird, mind blowing, surreal, stressful, exciting, anxiety provoking (although I didn't know I had anxiety back then, but well duh), and fun. It was all the feels.

My girls and I also joked a lot about this (meaning this new huge thing in my life) being an Oprah moment, not a Geraldo moment. As in the big reveal and how amazing it was. It was so cool and surreal. It was so many things. But it was beautiful cool not, shock and awe and drama cool.

My dad paid for a ticket to fly me to San Diego to meet him. I went with my new brother who had had a challenging relationship with him, but a relationship regardless.

He was in a hospice in San Diego in the Mission District in a wing that was designated for caring and holding space for AIDS patients at that time in their lives. He'd arranged for a car to pick us up at the airport and then drive us immediately to him.

When we got to the hospice, my first visual inside the building was of Joan Croc of McDonald's fame. Her portrait was in the main area, due to her financial donation and support for the organization.

We were then escorted by a staff member who walked down the hall with us to take us to my dad's room.

I remember talking to my brother about him "going in first," meaning into my dad's room before me. We'd never laid eyes on each other and I remember starting to feel very anxious, butterflies, and all the things.

Can you imagine laying eyes on one of your parents for the first time? Well, I'm sure some of you can… I really wish I could go back and witness this as that proverbial "fly on the wall." That would be, well, that would be fascinating.

When we got to his room, my brother went in and said hi. I could hear them talking. I stood just outside of the doorway, so I couldn't be seen.

When it was my turn to go in and meet him, I stepped in the middle of the doorway. He was sitting in a wheelchair in the middle of the door just a few inches inside the door. He was smiling. Maybe he was grinning. I'm not really sure.

So here's the interesting thing. As I've said before, things were fuzzy. The plane ride from Minneapolis to San Diego. The car ride from the airport. Getting out of the car and into the hospice. But seeing him for the first time is forever burned into my brain.

Seeing him for the first time, I froze. I physically froze. I was also speechless.

I couldn't move. I couldn't move my feet. I couldn't talk. I was frozen. My eyes worked. My ears worked. I could hear and see just fine. I just couldn't move my body or my mouth.

He was wearing a royal blue warm up (sweats and a matching jacket and a white tee). He was thin. He was bald. He had spots on his bald head.

I'm pretty sure the first thing he said to me was, "Come here girl."

I think I tried, but it took a minute before I could actually move.

When I was able to, I walked in and hugged him. He stayed in the chair. His friend was there, his girlfriend's cousin, Berto.

There were four of us in the room.

Dad got back into bed.

I looked around at the room. He had the pictures of me I'd sent in a frame. He told me I looked like the actress Rachel Ward. I had short, tight hair in the photo (high school senior headshot). I took it as a compliment because I knew exactly who she was. I was a huge fan of the movie *The Thorn Birds* that she starred in. Oh, and yes, I had read the book, in case you're wondering. It was beautiful.

We were in the room and I remember I kept staring at him. As if it were a dream. He kept staring at me, too.

Shortly after he sent us down to the gift shop to get some food and then back to his house to unpack our things.

For the next few days, we (my brother and I) were in and out of his house, back and forth to the hospice, meeting people, talking, laughing, it was so much new. It was amazing.

I not only met my dad for the first time. I also got to spend time at his house. I was with his two dogs. I saw his things. I learned what type of music he liked. He liked a lot of music and had a lot of CDs, mainly jazz. Smooth jazz.

I saw my picture in his house.

I saw he liked plants.

I saw he liked food (ha, he had cookbooks).

I saw he had massive amounts of alcohol, even though he didn't drink (this was discussed in one of our letters).

I saw he collected things like oversized dolls (the two-feet-tall ones) and decorative plates. I saw he collected Lladros.

He also smoked like a fiend. I remember thinking, no wonder he was dying of cancer. But, I was a closet smoker then too so how dare I judge?

Oh I can be judgey with the best of them. But you know what they say, right?

The next few days were so full.

We bonded. We laughed. We hugged a lot. I drank a lot of wine.

My uncle, his cousin, came from New York to see him.

I met his amazing beautiful girlfriend, Norma, and her two daughters. We bonded immediately almost as if we'd known each other forever. We spent time together talking and Norma was able to fill in a lot of the blanks regarding family and more.

We had a night out in Tijuana. We took Dad out to eat.

I met and talked to his doctors about his diagnosis. The word from the doctor was, "the horse was already out of the gate." Meaning he was diagnosed with prostate cancer and it was too late to do anything about it when he saw the doctor.

I also learned he "hated doctors."

I also learned he loved Kenny G.

That he'd only been back to Greece once since he left to come to the states with my mom in the 1960s.

He spoke five languages: Greek, English, French, and two others.

He was an artist (I saw and later found some of his artwork).

He…

It was a lot.

He asked me to help him go home so he could "die at home."

That was a little bit of work to make that happen. Both my brother and I did what was needed to get him to be able to go home, including a nurse, a hospital bed, and all the other necessary things.

We got him home.

We had his friends over at his request so he could see everyone "one more time." He was very real about his dying.

I remember sitting in his living room with all of these men I'd never met. Everyone was drinking. Everyone was laughing and sharing stories and telling me about him. A few of his guy friends, his girlfriend's cousin, Dad, and me. His girlfriend couldn't join us. It was fun.

At some point in this week, or whatever amount of time we were there, I also learned about him and his family, and became, "the oldest" who had to do all the death paperwork, met more of his friends, found we had a few things in common, talked about his relationship with my mom and…

Was offered a position at the university I had applied to just before I flew out to meet him. The week ended. I flew back to Wisconsin. I started my new job the following day.

It was winter and I drove 30 miles in the snow to meet my new colleagues in a parking lot to drive another hour to go to the work site (an underserved high school) and job shadow.

It feels like what I just said above is one of those super corny lines like, "I walked 10 miles to school uphill in the winter without shoes," or something like that.

But it's true. That all happened within a matter of two to three days.

I got the job offer while in San Diego. I accepted. I flew home. I started work.

Just like nothing happened.

That week my dad called me and asked me to come back. He asked me to move in with him. He said I could have the spare bedroom. That we could be together. He offered to buy my ticket and fly me out again so we could talk.

How in the world was I going to give up my life to be with him? I was 30, we'd only just met, and I'd barely started this amazing new job at the university.

I have to admit, after thinking about it, I knew I needed to go back and be with him. He was dying and we'd just met and we hit it off really well.

I'm very aware that I am lucky here. Meeting a birth parent for the first time for some is not always a good thing.

After discussing it with my mom, I called my colleague (the one who offered me the job) and told him my situation. He agreed he'd talk to our department chair and then get back to me on how, if at all, I could go and still have my job.

He (colleague and Director of Disability Services) soon became one of my favorite people ever. We figured I could go over a weekend and not risk losing my new job. I did. I got there on a Friday and was there alone with him and his nurses. Ruth and Denise.

This part again is fuzzy due to everything that went on and I'm pretty sure I didn't sleep for the next 48 hours.

Dad and I spent the next few days laughing, laying in his bed in his bedroom talking about his family. Me asking questions about people in the pictures in books. Him telling me I asked "too many questions."

We bonded even more.

He had a folie bag on (he had a catheter in) and had to go to the bathroom constantly. He thought he had to pee all the time, due to the prostate cancer, so I'd follow him in, carrying the bag and would sit on the floor while he argued about me giving him a cigarette. He'd fall asleep on the toilet while holding his cigarette. The cigarette would burn down. I'd take it from his fingers. I'd butt it out and he'd wake up, ask me for another cigarette and then we'd do this over and over.

We repeated this dance many times.

This pattern of being really awake and then being so wiped he'd barely be lucid, went on the whole weekend.

We watched female standup comedy. We laughed.

We watched *My Cousin Vinny*. We laughed more.

He then crashed and slept for hours. I was always afraid this would be it.

He rallied and on Saturday or Sunday morning I found him cleaning under his stove.

I scolded him. He replied with just as much snark. The nurse said this "was normal" and that it didn't really mean anything as far as him "getting better."

I talked to the nurses and more about how to help him due to the pain level.

By Sunday afternoon he'd declined even more and wasn't able to leave the hospital bed in his living room.

I layed in the bed with him all day.

He made some sounds. I watched TV.

On Sunday night some time in the middle of the night, he died. Two feet away from me.

I was sleeping on the couch next to the bed. I heard him. There were sounds. There was a gurgling sound that I was told by all the nurses that would happen. They call it the death rattle. Was new to me.

I immediately dialed 911. I'm not sure because I was a zombie and nothing was clear in my head.

I sat with him. It was eerily quiet. It was 2-something in the morning.

I hugged him.

The next thing I remember was two men showing up with a gurney to take him out and as they did....

I'm pausing here because only a few people know about this part of the story.

What I'm about to tell you as far as what happened next... happened. This I know in my bones and I still get emotional once in a while when I hear this song.

When they, the two men who took his body out on a gurney were leaving the house... the stereo turned on in the guest room and began to play Kenny G's song "Going Home."

I froze again. There was no one else in the house but me, Dad on the gurney, and the men taking him out. The nurse wasn't there and there absolutely wasn't anyone in the hall that led to that room where the stereo was.

The men took him out the opposite way of that room.

I was too blitzed to think anything other than that was dad telling me goodbye when he couldn't the last few hours we'd had together.

After that I never questioned it. I still don't.

The next few days again were a blur. I had to ask for time off with my new job so I could stay and take care of his things, a ceremony of some sort, wait for my brother to come back so we could pack, donate, and more.

The first night I was alone in the house, other weird things happened. And they kept on happening for almost a year. But regardless of what the weird things were, I knew it was him...

For the next few years, the weird things happened and the weird became not so weird. The chain of events that took place after meeting him anchored me and put me on a trajectory of having enough money to go to Greece for the first time to meet family, which led me to meet my first husband, which then gave me my girls.

It was a gift that keeps on giving.

It also led me to want to know more about family.

It led me to want to know more about how and why he was the way he was… Meaning… He was a talented and tortured soul who was raised without a father. He left Greece to what I can only believe was to come to the U.S. to become a star (this theory of mine based on a picture I have of him mugging and pretending to be James Dean on a beach in Egypt when he was 20-something, my uncle confirmed this).

Imagine coming to another country which you only know of from the movies. The climate is the polar opposite of where you were raised. Greece to St. Paul, Minnesota.

He was also gay. Or at least bisexual. There was a reason he was in the AIDS wing. But in the 60s when he arrived in this country… It was hidden. It had to be to keep people safe so they could love the ones they love and live their lives with some sense of realness.

Don't worry, I'm not planning to go into the history of LGBTQ. If you're curious, read about Harvey Milk. Watch *Pose* on Netflix. Ask someone. In those days "coming out" was, well you know….

I also know he was a tortured soul due to all the stories I was told about him by his girlfriend, his second ex-wife (my brother's mother), and the debris I found at his house when cleaning out his things.

He was married three or four times. My mom, the first. My brother's mom, the second. And another woman or two whose photos I found in his house.

I found letters he'd written to my brother's mother that were so mean I was shocked. They were not written by the man I met. They were written by a very angry and probably very very very drunk man based on what I read. They were mean horrific graphic letters and I still to this day don't know why I found them in an old suitcase in a closet at his house.

This was not the man I met who was kind, caring, curious, and giving. This was a different person. One whose life took turns that I'm sure he didn't plan on or couldn't have planned on.

I don't understand where the physically hurting someone else (him hurting my mom and I think my brother's mom) came in... clearly from somewhere. This is learned...

I do know that being raised by a single mom with his father out of the picture (even though apparently his mother kept a picture of his dad hanging in the kitchen) harmed him at some level.

I was told by my girls' Greek grandmother... it was translated for me... that in the 1960s being a single mom in Greece was viewed as very shameful (not acceptable). So he was then raised in a house where his mother was highly stressed and ashamed due to cultural norms. She died of stomach cancer right after I was born.

Just as him being absent in my life messed with me and I wasn't even aware of it until last week.

Yes, you saw that right.

Last week. When I'm writing this book.

The "aha" moment that I had last week was so profound and deep and "well duh" and "no seriously?" and "now I get it" that it made sense that it took me longer than planned for the first draft of this to be completed.

I needed another "aha" moment for this to come full circle. My point here is: he had his shit. Whatever that was. We all do. And his shit impacted me even though he was nowhere near me for 30 years of my life.

We were literally together in the same space for 13 days. Not enough time to "harm" me.

But his absence disrupted part of me.

This is why.

One of my teachers and favorite people in the world, Phyllis, who I've worked with for the last 25 years, helped me understand this; but I didn't really, and I mean really, get it until last week.

Stick with me because this will have many tendrils.

This is the nature versus nurture, epigenetic, generational trauma, woo-woo theory of mine.

- My dad was never part of my life
- My adopted father sexually assaulted me
- My mother was physically there, but never felt emotionally there for me
- Life happens – lawsuit with adopted father, college, car accidents, pregnancy, traumatic childbirth, miscarriages, divorces, losing a job, autoimmune disease, single parenting, single parenting two children with autoimmune, single parenting one daughter with a disability, COVID, etc.
- My mother's triggers are money and men ("swiss cheese" analogy)

Not only did my stress, tension, and traumas have a massive impact on me, but so did my father not being around.

For most of my life I felt off. Not whole. Like something was missing. Like something was not ok.

Yes! That's it exactly!

Like something was not ok and for most of my life I always felt like it was the sexual assault. Or my mom not being there for me or... any of the other things that happened to me.

When I realized recently that it was my dad missing from my life that bookended my whole story, that that was the missing piece of me. That that was why I've never felt like a whole person. Because that part of me was not around.

And I've been trying to figure out why I felt not ok. I've felt unwhole. Understanding how trauma segments us on a cognitive level is different than having a felt sense of it. Knowing and feeling are two different things. On an energetic level it was his energy that was missing. His presence. His... whatever.

Intellectually I knew this. Or so I thought. But still there was something simmering below the surface. That was the missing piece of the me puzzle and it took me 25 years to figure it out.

I've always said I was glad he was not around or part of my life because if he was I'm pretty sure I would have ended up in a different kind of hell than I pictured part of my life to be... regardless of how it looked or felt to everyone on the outside.

Because of course I don't mask.... ha! Me... yeah, right.

The twist with this is that as much as I felt him being part of my life would have made it much worse, it was also a gift that he wasn't around.

So which is it? Yes, I'm contradicting myself.

Was him being gone a good or bad thing?

I know it sounds like I'm saying it's both. And it is both.

His absence left a feeling of unwholeness. Which I wasn't able to deeply grasp until recently. Feeling unwhole or off my whole life.

However, had he been present, his trauma drama would have spilled over into my life and made things worse. I'm certain even with our brief time together that he had a long laundry list of his own shit... probably an alcoholic, angry, his own daddy and abandonment issues, attachment issues, etc.

I know I met him at just the right time for both of us... almost as if it were scripted that way... wink wink.

So yes, it is both bad and good, which is what life really is, right? It's the nature of how things work... we need both. Dark and light. Soft and hard. So what really is the point here? The point is that life is hard... at times. It's not fair. It sucks. We all have trauma. It's part of life.

I call it the trauma continuum.

On any given day each and every one of us is on that continuum. From small stressors to huge traumas.

It's how we navigate through. It's what we do with it. It's how we manage our shit. It's how we heal the hurts. It's the support we have. It's the tools we have. It's the tools we use. It's everything.

It's also life. It's messy. It's scary. It's dirty. It's stressful. It's traumatic.

It's also having an understanding of how shit works that helps. At least it's helped me.

I love learning. I love understanding how and why I've thought or felt or acted or said certain things and having a felt sense of "if this happened to you, this could explain things." Notice I said "could."

Because current trauma theory shares and you can pretty much find anywhere if you look, that trauma is not what happened, not the event, it was how it was received by the individual. By their system and how it was then navigated (handled, processed, etc.).

Again, I had all this shit happen to me but it wasn't what happened to me necessarily, it was how my nervous system (brain and spinal cord), my being, my body, my everything, received it and then either moved through (fight or flight) the stress and trauma or it got stuck (freeze, flood, dissociate and fawn) and stored in my being.

Now, let's put all of that together and bring in modern day science and neuroscience that supports my theory of using the body as part of the healing recipe.

The Importance of Using the Body to Heal

"We need to get out of our heads
and into our bodies.
We can't talk our way out of trauma."
- Christine Varnavas

P sychiatrist and author Dr. Bessel Van der Kolk, in his "bible for mental health," as one of my clients puts it, *The Body Keeps The Score*, identifies the importance of using the body to heal.

He details and explains how it is crucial to use the body (as opposed to talk therapy as a standalone) to help people truly heal. Or, as I call it, the Deep Dive into your own wellness (self care). He also explains why and gives us a breakdown of neuroanatomy (study of the structure and organization of the nervous system).

To paint a picture of what I was explaining before about how the brain works under stress and trauma, Dr. Van der Kolk describes how our "alarm system," our pre-built-in safety system (autonomic nervous system) behaves under stress and traumatic situations.

"Under normal conditions people react to a threat with a temporary increase in stress hormones. As soon as the threat is over, the hormones dissipate and the body returns to normal. The stress hormones of traumatized people, in contrast take much longer to return to baseline and spike quickly and disproportionality in response to mildly stressful stimuli. The insidious effects of constantly elevated stress hormones include:

memory and attention problems
irritability and sleep disorders
and other long term health issues"

In chapter four, "Anatomy of Survival," of his book Dr. Van der Kolk explains that,

"After trauma the world is experienced with a different nervous system. A survivor's energy now becomes focused on suppressing inner chaos at the expense of spontaneous involvement in their lives."

"These attempts to maintain control over unbearable physiological reactions can result in a whole range of physical symptoms… fibromyalgia, CFS (chronic fatigue syndrome), autoimmune."

Dr. Van der Kolk is giving words to why using the body to heal is paramount. Because if the body is not part of the healing and wellness plan… past hurts, stress, and trauma, and current and future stress and trauma may, if it hasn't already, lead to disease.

For those of us who are "me too"s, sexual assault survivors, this quote from the same chapter is, in my mind, speaking directly to us:

> "Being able to move and do something different to protect yourself is a critical factor in determining whether or not a horrible experience will leave long lasting scars."

In my case when I was being assaulted, I froze. I didn't know what was going on, at least not the first time. I froze as my brilliant brain and strong body knew what to do to keep me safe. I also dissociated by looking at and focusing on the noise of the air conditioning and the heater. Again, all by brilliant design. My system knew exactly what it needed to do at that moment because I couldn't fight back or run away.

I could not move. And as the quote above says, "being able to move..." I was not able to move. I froze, and because I froze, the shit (the story, the experience, the memory, the emotions, the energy) stayed in my body.

And since it stayed in my body, every time as I got older and life continued to happen as it does, and I experienced some other flavor of stress or trauma, and I was unable to release the stress chemicals, it compounded things.

In my words. There's only so much a body can take before it says "Nope, I'm done."

I'm done meaning because we still have to survive and function in our crazy busy life (this is my body and all its internal systems talking)... I will function, but I will function differently because parts of us are on overdrive all the time and the other parts can't keep up so we have to adapt to this new way of stressedoutness and we weren't designed to do all this all the time. We are way out of balance.

Hang on. Let me explain.

Dr. Porges' work that talks about the autonomic nervous system (safety system) and how it behaves behind the scenes without awareness reinforces my "knowing" that, due to my alarm bells and whistles going off all the time behind the scene, my system finally had to say "No, I can't do this anymore." Because it was on high alert all the time, dumping stress chemicals and looking for cues of safety and always controlling my environment so there would be no surprises, it was exhausted and overworked so my body talked to me by....

1. Certain body parts that were touched during the assaults went into a freeze and did not work as designed. How do I know this? For years, and I mean years, when I was working out – either teaching a class or working out – my hamstrings, inner thigh muscles, and glutes would not respond. It was almost as if the muscle was not there at all. I would have to work extra hard to even get the muscle fibers to fire (work or respond to a stress or a stretch). As I mentioned earlier, those are the places that my abuser touched so many years ago.

2. My stomach around the C-section scar, the entire area near it: front, back, left, and right sides are always either numb or tight and in pain (more on this below).

3. The autoimmune disease Graves was the culmination of too much stress on my body.

This is how my body kept the score. I also believe these parts are holding fear and sadness. Why wouldn't they? At least the sexual assault and the first C-section. Both were fear based experiences.

Neither time did I know what was going on – the first time he messed with me and the first C-section. Since both things happened more than once, the second time for each I pretty much had a good idea of what was going to happen or maybe what to expect.

This is also how my body talks to me...

During one of my morning personal practice sessions, it came to me that the reason I couldn't feel my stomach and I had to work wicked hard to do core work after my C-section and my low back hurts off and on almost debilitatingly, was because it's just as much emotional as it is physical (structural).

The C-section Scare

This might get a little woo woo for some of you and no, the above is not a typo…

For the last 20 plus years, my stomach from my belly button down to my pubic bone has felt numb or dead and my low back has chronically hurt.

Of course it makes sense that due to physical trauma to that area (emergency C-section scar running up and down not left to right – if you aren't familiar with this lovely version of an incision) in the front of my body… it makes sense that that area would be "dead." I'm not a surgeon, obviously, but I would assume that there was maybe some nerve damage and other tissue that was affected long term. The incision is not a straight line. It's wavy and has interesting lines around it. It begins at my belly button, curves down to the right, and then ends up going to the left. The skin pulls right. It pulls left. It's all over the place. My abs have never been the same again.

It was also an incision that was made as a result of the doctors saving my and my oldest daughter's lives. I know on the medical side of it they were doing their job. Saving our lives and delivering her into this world. For this, I am grateful. They saved us. Thank you! Whoever you were.

The other side of this, is that on my end it was immediate fear. Plain and simple fear. The fear of being told by the doctor that if I didn't reply "yes" to his question immediately we could both die. That's fear. Actually that's more than fear, that's terror. I know what fear feels like. That was shock and terror all in one nano second.

So it makes sense to me then that there is fear and sadness in that part of my body. It also makes sense to me that it is frozen from fear and sadness and pain.

Our bodies, our muscles, our cells have emotions.

One of my teachers of over 25 years, Phyllis, who you've heard me mention before, shared that "every cell in our body has consciousness." I love this! I've also seen something similar in print from Deepak Chopra.

That goes hand in hand with emotions. Why would it not? You've heard the term "muscle memory" right? Best example... the "It's just like riding a bike" idiom. You can take a break from doing something for years (like riding a bike) and then get on even decades later and your body still knows how to do it.

How can that be just rote memory? I don't believe it.

I believe that it's part rote memory, but it's emotional, too. Why? Here's why...

Is it such a stretch to think that muscles and body parts have emotions? If inanimate manmade objects hold memories for people, why is it impossible for muscles, bones, fascia, and other body parts that are part of our being to have emotions, too?

Think about someone who has passed who you loved so deeply. Think about how their things, maybe a grandma's favorite blanket or tea cup or something, sparks emotion for you. That's an inanimate object that triggers emotion.

Or you still have a piece of furniture or something that was an ex-husband's thing and it still irritates you to have it in your space.

I believe that every part of us feels things and has memories.

I also believe that if our parents, grandparents, great grandparents, great great grandparents, and another ton of generations back, didn't heal or have the opportunity to heal for whatever reason, they passed it on to us.

How could they not?

Think about character traits, hobbies, likes, habits that are passed down from generation to generation with

https://www.nature.com/articles/d41586-022-01626-x

no basis in your current reality. There is also evidence out there that proves this isn't so woo woo. A study published in the journal Nature Neuroscience adds to a growing pile of evidence suggesting that characteristics outside of the strict genetic code may also be acquired from our parents through epigenetic inheritance.

"Smell is very deeply ingrained in our emotional memory," says Eric Vermetten, a clinical psychiatrist and trauma researcher at Leiden University Medical Center in the Netherlands.*

If the function of the nose can induce emotions, why can't muscles and other parts of the body induce and even hold emotions?

I don't believe the saying a broken heart is just metaphorical or structural.

Final Call To Action

At this time of cultural awakening, the "me too" movement, failing patriarchal systems, increased racial wars, and as author Resmaa Menakem of *My Grandmother's Hands*, states, a "reckoning." I charge you to embrace radical and deep, delicious healing. It's time to stop being afraid of the deep dive that the future of our world requires and start healing the ruptures in the fabric of each of us. It takes work and it is doable.

Accept that trauma happens. It's happened since the beginning of time. We also have to flip the paradigm as women and take care of ourselves first. This means doing the work for ourselves and stopping the cycle of generational trauma by unknowingly passing it on to those we love. We don't have the luxury of not doing the work!

We are carrying around not only our personal traumas in this lifetime in this body. But we are also carrying around possibly countless years of unprocessed trauma from our ancestors. There is no blame here. There is no shame here. Now we know and we have to do better.

I would use the word "ask" here, but that seems too passive. This is a **call to action** to heal your shit NOW, with the tools that work best for you. Get into your body and out of your head. Do the work. Move. Laugh. Breath. Find your happy and create a future that feels more like love and less like fear.

Ultimately, healing is a very personal journey. Parts of it are similar and maybe familiar for all of us, acceptance and understanding, grieving and forgiving, laughing and crying. It takes time. It takes patience. It takes tools. It takes two steps forward and then three steps back. It's not linear. It's messy. It's scary. It's beautiful.

The biggest gift you can give to the entire world is you healing you. I do this work for me, my children, my mother, my grandmother, and everyone of my ancestors because the vibration of healing happens in all directions. The energy of healing is powerful. Take your power and use it for good because there is wisdom in trauma… it makes you uniquely you.

If I can do this… so can you.

Education is power.

Movement is freedom.

Combined together they will move us forward so we can break the cycle of generational trauma and heal. So here's to us… to our collective healing.

Being a cycle breaker starts with the body. Getting into our bodies and parsing through all the love and the muck.

Healing generational trauma means healing in this body, on this planet. Right now!

You have the power to change things!

Find what works for you, heal your shit and have fun doing it…

To end with a fun note…

One of my favorite quotes from my mother
(as this book is about getting into your body to heal) is

"Most of my life I didn't even know I had a body,
I just felt like I was a floating around head."

Insert nod and smile…

Let's leave a legacy of love not fear for future generations.

Much love,

Christine

One Last Thing

As I come to the end of writing this I'm still curious and still learning. I'm still doing the work. I noticed I was getting frustrated with myself that as I would give myself a deadline to "be done," something, some life-thing would happen and it would push out my writing and my end date. But, per my usual, every time my "done date" had come and gone, there was some new golden nugget of relevant material or a story or something that would show up that needed to be in this book. Once again the universe has my back… grateful!

The last golden nugget that showed up was information that I felt was necessary to add due to the "scientific proof" or "evidence based" necessity… However I was not willing to re-write or add to a chapter, so…

The golden nugget came in the form of the "proof" that I've been looking for regarding the science behind how trauma is passed down as opposed to "I just know." I recently signed up for a Trauma Super Conference online.

Yes, I'm a trauma geek. One of the presenters, Dr. Arielle Schwartz, licensed clinical psychologist, author, wife, and mother, shared her thoughts on how generational trauma is passed down.

When asked by the host of the conference, "How transgenerational trauma is passed on?" She shared…
"In several ways,

1.   **Epigenetics**
The research of the changes at the cellular level, how our body processes cortisol and the shaping of our nervous system, and how changes with the mother get passed to a child. Children can be born with a predisposition to higher sensitivity to stress and that this is profoundly common.

2.   **Embodiment**
There is no standard definition of this, however it basically means using the body, its senses, its mannerisms, voice intonation, etc. We embody what we are around. Nature versus nurture. We absorb what we are around… habits, speech patterns, etc."

The beauty of this is knowing this is real. There is science and research behind this. However, the downside or danger of knowing is that once we know we can be too harsh on ourselves. We can blame and shame ourselves for not doing better or not knowing.

Awareness is the first step. Acceptance is the second… that we all inherited things from our ancestors… the good, the bad, and the other. Action is the third. It's our responsibility to step up, to learn, to do the work, do good work, and be gentle with ourselves and others because now we know.

One of the outcomes of writing this (my mother fact checked for me) is recently learning that my grandmother did not allow my mother to be alone in the same space with her father, mom's grandfather. Oh really? The stories are continuing to surface and my curiosity tells me that there may be another book in the future… hmmmm.

> *"Sometimes our bodies carry legacy wounds from our family lineage. This intergenerational trauma is the unresolved trauma that has been passed down across generations and, if left unaddressed, it might diminish your ability to breathe deeply, move freely, take up space, or use your voice."*
> Dr. Arielle Schwartz

A big part of the work I do with my students and my clients is to create a foundational awareness of the wicked wisdom of the body. To acknowledge and fully appreciate it. To stay curious. To learn to trust it.

Take the time to be with yourself and all the magical messy parts that make up the amazing you.

A beautiful women I met said this to me
and then followed it up by..."and I mean that in the nice way."

Glossary

ACEs - The CDC-Kaiser Permanente adverse childhood experiences (ACE) study is one of the largest investigations of childhood abuse and neglect and household challenges and later-life health and well-being.*

Ahimsa - nonviolence, not hurting any being including ourselves

Autonomic Nervous System - a component of the peripheral nervous system that regulates involuntary physiologic processes including heart rate, blood pressure, respiration, digestion and sexual arousal.

Dissociation - a disconnection between a person's thoughts, memories, feelings, actions or sense of who he or she is. This is a normal process that everyone has experienced. Examples of mild, common dissociation include daydreaming, highway hypnosis or "getting lost" in a book or movie, all of which involve "losing touch" with awareness of one's immediate surroundings. During a traumatic experience such as an accident, disaster or crime victimization, dissociation can help a person tolerate what might otherwise be too difficult to bear. **

* https://www.cdc.gov/violenceprevention/aces/about.html
** https://www.psychiatry.org/patients-families/dissociative-disorders/what-are-dissociative-disorders

Epigenetics - the study of changes in organisms caused by modification of gene expression, rather than alteration of the genetic code itself.

Functional Freeze - is one of several defense responses to trauma, state of paralysis.***

Interoception - understanding our internal state

Neuroception - our body scanning our environment for cue's of safety

Numbing - is mostly unconsciously trying to avoid uncomfortable emotions with a variety of behaviors (drinking, drugs, shopping, always being busy and more)

Polyvagal Theory - the science of safety and connection by Dr. Stephen Porges

Self Regulation - ability to manage ourselves, to have an awareness of when enough is enough without the help of others

Svadhyaya - self study

*** https://www.nicabm.com/topic/freeze/

Resources
Stay Curious &
Dig Deeper

BOOKS

Eastern Body Western Mind - Anodea Judith
I Know Why The Caged Bird Sings - Dr. Maya Angelou
Living, Loving, Learning - Dr. Leo Buscaglia
Light on Yoga - B.K.S. Iyengar
Miss America by Day - Marilyn van DerBur
Mother Hunger - Kelly McDaniel
My Grandmother's Hands - Resmaa Menakem
Peace Is Every Step - Thich Nhat Hanh
The Body Keeps the Score - Dr. Bessel van der Kolk
The Heart of Yoga - T.K.V. Desikachar
The Post Traumatic Growth Guidebook - Dr. Arielle Schwartz
The Power of Intention - Wayne Dyer
What Happened to You? - Oprah Winfrey, Dr. Bruce Perry
When Things Fall Apart - Pema Chodron
You Are a Badass - Jen Sincero

PEOPLE & ORGANIZATIONS

Deb Dana
Dr. Arielle Schwartz
Dr. Dan Siegel
Dr. David Berceli
Dr. Jaiya John
Dr. Gabor Maté
Dr. Stephen Porges
Mental Health News Radio
Mental Wellness for Mom's (insta)
Laughter Online University
Laughter Yoga
NAMI (National Alliance on Mental Illness)
NICABM (National Institute for The Clinical
         Application of Behavioral Medicine)
RAINN (Rape Abuse & Incest National Network)
PTSD.gov (Post Traumatic Stress Disorder.gov)
The Breathe Network
The Mighty (app)
The Real Depression Project (insta)
The Trauma Steward Institute
Traumageek.com
Yoga Journal
Yoga International

ARTICLES & RESOURCES

Cracked Up (movie)
https://www.crackedupmovie.com

When Trauma Gets Stuck In the Body
https://www.psychologytoday.com/us/blog/in-the-body/201910/when-trauma-gets-stuck-in-the-body

Why Exercise is So Crucial for Maintaining Mental Health
https://www.psychologytoday.com/us/blog/what-works-and-why/201803/why-exercise-is-so-crucial-maintaining-mental-health

Sensitive The Untold Story (documentary)
https://sensitivethemovie.com

The Wisdom of Trauma (documentary)
https://thewisdomoftrauma.com

Laughter Articles
Laughter really is among the best medicines, says Air Force nurse
https://www.health.mil

Laughter Is the Best Medicine
https://www.psychiatrictimes.com/view/laughter-best-medicine

Laughter Online University
offers free online sessions weekly
https://www.laughteronlineuniversity.com

Laughter Yoga
offers free online sessions weekly
https://www.laughteryoga.org/

Radio Program
Laughter: The Best Medicine (48 minutes)
https://www.npr.org/2020/09/25/916997530/laughter-the-best-medicine

YOGA RESOURCES

Dr. Arielle Schwartz (live and virtual)
https://drarielleschwartz.com/therapeutic-yoga-classes-in-boulder/

Andrea Gerisimo (live and virtual)
http://thirdmountain.com/yogaclasses.html

Bonnie Pariser (live and virtual)
https://www.yoga-loka.com

Sadie Nardini (online)
https://sadienardini.com

TRE® RESOURCES
About TRE®
www.traumaprevention.com

Dr. Berceli Resources
Youtube: https://www.youtube.com/@davidberceli
Books:
- *Shake It Off Naturally: Reduce Stress, Anxiety & Tension with TRE*
- *The Revolutionary Trauma Release Process*
- *Trauma Releasing Exercises*

Cartoon Video explaining TRE®
https://www.youtube.com/watch?v=1PT1crBhhUE

About the Author

Christine Varnavas is an educator, author, speaker, mother, a TRE® Global Certification Trainer, a Women's Wellness Advisor, and a childhood sexual abuse survivor. Her passion for movement, laughter, and fun has fueled her teaching and training for over 30 years where she's helped countless women globally to feel better in their skin and raise their resilience. She invites you to fall in love with taking care of yourself.

You can learn more about Christine, her work, and more at christinevarnavas.com

Made in the USA
Monee, IL
19 June 2023